GRIEF

...AS A SECOND LANGUAGE®

A GUIDEBOOK FOR SURVIVING THE LOSS OF A LOVED ONE

STACY PARKER

EDITED AND FOREWORD BY
VALERIE ALEXANDER

Grief as a Second Language
Copyright © 2018 by Valerie Alexander and Stacy Parker

Published by
Speak Happiness Press
www.SpeakHappiness.com

This book is available in print and as an eBook.

Author Photo of Stacy Parker by Robin Aronson
Author Photo of Valerie Alexander by Samantha Simmonds Ronceros
Cover Design by Valerie Alexander
Cover Layout by Hillary Hafke
Interior Design by Ramesh Kumar Pitchai

ISBN-13: 978-1725918894
ISBN-10: 1725918897

This book is lovingly dedicated to my beautiful daughter, Alyssa, who taught me about life and love…

I am standing upon the seashore.
A ship, at my side, spreads her white sails to the morning breeze and starts for the blue ocean.
She is an object of beauty and strength.
I stand and watch her until, at length, she hangs like a speck of white cloud just where the sea and sky come to mingle with each other.

Then, someone at my side says, "There... she is gone."

Gone where?

Gone from my sight.
That is all.
She is just as large in mast, hull and spar as she was when she left my side.
And, she is just as able to bear her load of living freight to her destined port.
Her diminished size is in me — not in her.

And, just at the moment when someone says, "There, she is gone," there are other eyes watching her coming, and other voices ready to take up the glad shout, "Here she comes!"

And that is dying…

— Henry Van Dyke

TABLE OF CONTENTS

FOREWORD

By Valerie Alexander

"Don't ever let anyone tell you how to grieve."

Those were the magic words that helped me through what was, up to that point, the saddest period of my life.

I was 29 years old and had just lost both my grandparents in a period of two days. My grandmother had been my closest friend. She was my rock, my 2:00 am phone call (the woman never slept), and the only person in my life who just listened when I needed someone to.

And then she was gone.

It was amazingly lucky, I suppose, to have made it to 29 without having suffered a major loss. But after their funeral, when I returned to the small house in Oakland that I lived in by myself, with my dog, I didn't really know what to do with the feelings I was experiencing. One day, I was sitting on my front porch steps, watching the dog play in the yard, and my neighbor from across the street walked over and sat next to me.

She was only a few years older and we didn't know each other that well, but she'd heard from another neighbor what had happened and asked how I was doing. I started to cry, then apologized for it, and that's when she said it:

"Don't ever let anyone tell you how to grieve."

She told me not to apologize. Then she told me not to try to control anything I was going to feel for the next several years. Yes...*years*. She described grief to me in a way that made it okay for me to deal with everything I never thought I'd experience. Honestly, I thought losing a loved one was something you got sad about for a while and then moved on. She smiled and shared that it didn't work that way at all.

She told me about losing her husband, unexpectedly, when their son was still very young, and how her response to grief was to crawl into a bottle. As a result, she almost lost everything. She shared how much work it took to get back to a life she could live, and she wanted to make sure I wouldn't make those same mistakes.

JoAnn, wherever you are, please know that I will always be grateful for the words and story you shared with me that day. You got me through not only that loss, but the much more devastating one I would suffer thirteen years later when the desperately wanted, already named little girl in my womb "failed to thrive" (the official medical term for it) and never had the chance to meet her dad or me.

When I lost my grandparents, I didn't know how important it was to have someone sit next to you and tell you what to expect and get you through your grief, but I know now. Which is why it was such a blessing that Stacy Parker and I were seated at the same table at a charity event last summer.

At that point, I had been the creator, editor and publisher of the "…as a Second Language" self-help and personal growth books for more than five years, with four titles in print (Happiness, Success, Parenting and Creativity) and several more in the pipeline, but it had never occurred to me how badly a book on this topic might be needed. Five minutes into speaking with Stacy about her work as a grief counselor, it became completely clear. It was imperative that this book exist. I asked if she wanted to write it, and the next morning got an email from her asking when she should start.

Like the other authors in this series, Stacy has been a dream to work with. That will always be universally true because the authors who are not a dream to work with (and there have been those) never quite make it to the finish line. Stacy, on the other hand, raced there.

With the first chapter she sent me, I knew this was going to be another shining jewel in the "…as a Second Language" series. The tone was exactly right – it felt like a dear friend sitting next to you, holding your hand, guiding you and letting you know everything was going to be alright. With each successive section she sent, it grew more and more into a work that anyone, regardless of the depth of their grief or the length of time since their loss, would be able to use to get through the toughest times.

If you're reading it now, there is probably a reason, and if so, I'm so sorry for your loss. The pages that follow are sure to provide comfort, solace and gentle guidance, just as my neighbor did, sitting with me on my porch, all those years ago.

Thank you for letting us be part of your journey.

And now, I hand you over to Stacy...

INTRODUCTION

LEARNING TO SPEAK THE LANGUAGE OF GRIEF

I am an expert on grief. My own experience has made me learn more about this subject than I ever wanted. Not only have I lost my father, a very close aunt, all my grandparents, and a couple of friends, I have also lost a child. Losing a child is what changed my life forever.

My daughter died over 20 years ago and I consider myself an expert now because I have learned how to live without her…something I never, ever thought possible. It is by far the hardest thing I have had to do in my life, but if I can survive and get past the intense, relentless, paralyzing pain that goes along with grief, and learn to be happy, grateful and more present in my life, then I believe anyone can, including you.

As a bereaved parent, I learned an enormous amount about experiencing grief, but the expertise in dealing with it came from eventually using my pain to become actively involved in grief support work and advocacy.

My husband and I began attending a local meeting of The Compassionate Friends ("TCF") for support. They are a national organization for bereavement assistance after someone loses a child, grandchild or sibling. We later facilitated the group for five years. In 2004 we co-chaired the TCF National Conference in Hollywood, California, with more than 1,100 people in attendance.

I am currently on the board of the Children's Hospice of America Foundation, which raises money and awareness nationally for palliative care and children's hospice programs throughout the country.

I've served as a parent advocate and educator on the Pediatric Palliative care board at Cedars Sinai Medical Center, the Comfort Care board at UCLA Mattel Children's Hospital, and have spoken at a number of IPPC - Initiative for Pediatric Palliative Care - conferences to provide the parent voice for the medical staff on how to better support families when their child becomes critically ill or dies. I have spoken to groups of medical residents and end-of-life nurses, helping them understand the parent's perspective.

I continue to work to support those actively grieving, having co-run a support group at Our House in Los Angeles for 4-7 year old children who lost a parent, and am a 'go-to" resource for friends and people in our community who have lost a family member or friend. I meet with them or talk on the phone, listening, guiding and referring them to different organizations for support, as needed.

This book is about getting through the depths of grief so you can find purpose, joy and love after a profound loss. You could have lost a friend, a parent, grandparent, a sibling, spouse or a child. The process is generally the same. Although most people believe the idea of losing a child is more painful than losing anyone else close to you (and since I did lose a child, I tend to agree), that is not to say losing any loved one is easy. The pain of a loss can, and probably will be excruciating for most people for a long while. Depending on the relationship you had with your loved one and your own experiences and sensitivities, a variety of things will determine how each death affects you.

Unfortunately there is no getting around grief easily. You have to go through it, deal with the feelings that come up and find a way to get to the other side. The steps we'll talk about here don't go in any particular order, but there are some guidelines we will go over, so you know what to expect. Each person is on their own schedule for the amount of time it will take for the pain of grief to subside. It depends on your beliefs, your capacity to handle stress, your support system and a little bit of giving yourself permission to feel better. This timeline is different for everyone.

Don't ever let anyone tell you it is time to be "over" your loss. When people asked me a year after my daughter's death if I was feeling better, I thought they were insane! They had no idea my journey was just beginning. A year is nothing! Two or five years is nothing! Not that you won't have happiness for that amount of time, but it can still be excruciatingly painful for years.

I am not sure how it happens, but somehow, with time, we just learn to live with the pain we carry. It may be just under the surface or feel like it is always there, but it does change over time.

That's not to say time heals. It's just that one day, you will realize you only cried once that day, or you laughed really hard with someone, or you really took in the beauty of where you were and had the feeling of being grateful.

Grief is a long, painful process, but somehow we all get through the worst of it. Never did I imagine I would, but I did…and so will you.

MY PERSONAL JOURNEY
A SUDDEN IMMERSION COURSE IN GRIEF

I got married when I was 25 years old and always knew I wanted to have kids. My husband and I planned for our first child with eager anticipation and I was lucky enough to get pregnant easily. I loved being pregnant! It felt like such a miracle that a life could grow inside me and as I got bigger and the baby started kicking, my husband and I were in awe and so excited.

I was a healthy 28-year-old and had a great pregnancy. I did pregnancy yoga and stayed away from sushi and hot dogs. I took really good care of myself. I remember going to my twenty week ultrasound and the radiologist told me, "Congratulations! You are going to have a healthy baby."

To be honest, I didn't think another thing about it. If the doctor told me the baby was healthy, then yay for me...all was well. Plus, all my friends were having babies and no one had any problems. I just figured it would be okay because it was okay for everyone else. Why wouldn't it be perfect? That's the way it should be, right?

I delivered a beautiful baby girl at 38 weeks with no complications and all was good with the world. She slept in my room that first night and I held her a lot and tried to feed her. I couldn't take my eyes off her. Nine hours after my daughter was born and had gone back to the nursery so I could shower in the morning, the nurses noticed her lips were turning blue. Suddenly, unbeknownst to me, the chaos began. They rushed her to the NICU (neonatal intensive care unit) and from there they started detecting problems that were yet to be determined.

A cardiologist finally came to our room to talk to us about our daughter's status. They had detected a severe heart defect and were in agreement that she needed surgery. They also discovered she had a bowel obstruction and with the additional issue, the hospital decided she would be better off at UCLA Medical Center, where they could handle all of this.

That first night, 18 hours after she was born, they transported my daughter by ambulance to the NICU at UCLA. Those 13.2 miles were the longest drive of my life. At just two days old, she had surgery on her bowel to fix the blockage. When she came out of surgery she was covered from head to toe with tubes and equipment and she had a tiny ileostomy bag. To say my husband and I were in shock and devastated is putting it mildly. We didn't realize it then, but we began at that moment to grieve the loss of not having a healthy child. We had no idea how much more grief was to come.

Before my daughter came out of surgery, we really didn't know what to expect, but from that point on, we were in for a rough ride. That was the first glimmer into what kind of pain was going to lay ahead. To see your newborn baby lying there surrounded by medical staff and hooked up to equipment…there are just no words to describe that pain. Our friends were all having happy, healthy babies, so we were also very aware of how our lives could have gone. But God had other plans for us.

My daughter stayed in the NICU for one month and one day. Her body was not ready for heart surgery yet, and because she was not able to fully eat orally they had put in an intravenous line to administer part of her nutrition. The nurses showed me how to change her dressings and tap the bubbles out of the TPN (total parenteral nutrition) line. I also learned how to change her ileostomy bag. This was definitely not something I ever thought I would know anything about. I was at the hospital all day, every day learning how to take care of my daughter and just holding her. That was the first new language I learned - pediatric nursing.

And then there was the general hospital language and learning to be an advocate for someone. That's an important lesson for everyone to learn because you know your family member best and the medical staff can make mistakes. It happens all the time.

We took my daughter home when she was one month and one day old and still on TPN. Luckily, we had nursing a few days a week, but I was terrified every time I was alone with her that I would do something wrong with her line and kill her. There were so many rules about caring for her. I just didn't want to make a mistake.

My daughter began itching when she was just a month or two old because her liver wasn't breaking things down in her blood. The nurses called it an "internal itch." She could never get relief from scratching but she would still scratch and scratch. I used to put socks on her hands to try to keep her from scratching herself too much. I would help her scratch and as she cried, I sobbed. There is nothing worse than seeing your child in pain and uncomfortable with nothing you can do to help her. It was a horribly helpless feeling.

I took her to doctors, specialists, healers, acupuncturists and chiropractors. I tried everything to make her comfortable. She also had appointments with our pediatrician, the cardiologist, the GI specialist and later the nephrologist (kidney specialist). When my daughter was three months old, she went back into the hospital again to have her bowel reconnected. During surgery they did a biopsy of her liver and guessed at that time that she had a rare disease called Alagille Syndrome. For the doctors, this diagnosis was just a guess, because the geneticists had not yet detected the mutation in the gene that proves this. Because of this we treated her as if she had this syndrome. It was all we could do.

When she was a year old we were told she was also in kidney failure. There were more doctor appointments, more medicine, and a lot more grieving on our part. During the time my daughter was alive, my mother was the only one who ever asked me what we thought we would do if my daughter died. At first I was angry with her. *What kind of question was that?*

I eventually realized she was asking me out of love and concern for my future, but on a day-to-day basis, I just thought about keeping my daughter comfortable and happy. That literally took up all my time and energy. In the two years she was alive, I didn't have time to think about the unthinkable. I also couldn't let myself go to that place of imagining life without her. It was just too much to bear. I literally thought, "If she dies, I will die! I can't live without her…"

When my daughter was two years, two months old, she had a seizure that turned out to be a blood clot in her brain. The doctors told us she had to have surgery right away because at the time they thought the blood clot was an infection. She went in for emergency surgery to remove the clot and during surgery her heart stopped beating and they couldn't revive her. The doctors came out just like in those horrible hospital shows to tell us she had died. Except this was real life. This was my life!

How could this be my life? It didn't feel real. My initial response after the doctors came out was to go into shock. I started shaking uncontrollably and I think I left my body for those first few days and sort of hovered above. I could feel my heart beating, but I felt hollow and numb. I moved, but with so much effort, and when people talked to me it felt like they were talking from the other side of a long tube. Everything felt slowed down and my head and heart were so heavy I didn't think I could carry them along with me.

I didn't cry at first. It all just felt so surreal. But when I finally did, I didn't stop crying for probably two years. The tears just kept coming and coming. It wasn't constant for two years but it was like a lightswitch. I could start at any time.

About a month after my daughter died, I started getting panic attacks. It was the first time in my life I had to go on medication to function. It felt like my body had just forgotten how to breathe. It was a horrible and scary feeling to not be able to take a breath and it became much worse at night. Grief is painful...emotionally and physically, and it hangs on for a long time.

I am not sure how much time it took for me to start to feel like myself again...for that pain in my heart to lessen. It was a very gradual thing for me. The first year was excruciating. Having to go through holidays and events for the first time was awful. The second year might have been worse because the numbness had started to wear off a bit.

But I would have short glimpses of feeling normal.

And life just goes on.

And you move with it because there is not another choice.

That pain I carried for so long is still always there, but normally it is tucked away somewhere in my body or my brain and only shows itself once in a while. I can access it any time though, especially when I meet someone newly bereaved. My heart can remember the pain like it was yesterday.

I'm so sorry if you are bereaved. I'm sorry for any grief you may be experiencing, whether recent or from decades ago. Together, we will explore some practical ways to get through some of the hardest parts of grief. And please don't ever forget — you have to give yourself time, patience and love.

This might be the hardest thing you will ever have to do.

So, take it slow and take care of yourself.

I'm here for you.

CHAPTER 1

DEFINING YOUR GRIEF

People can grieve many things in their lives. The loss of a job or a home, the break-up of a relationship or friendship, a change in their lives that can't be controlled. But the grief we are talking about in this book is related to the death of a loved one. Everyone at one time or another will grieve the loss of a loved one because everyone will die. It's a part of life and in recognizing that, hopefully we can understand that all the feelings that come with losing a loved one are normal and expected.

The dictionary's definition of grief is the deep sorrow that is caused by someone's death. In my opinion that definition is an understatement. After my daughter died, I wanted to die too. I felt numb and overwhelmed, hopeless and lost. The literal pain that settled in my heart was so heavy and so painful, each breath felt difficult to take.

Support and love are needed to get through the worst of it, but no one can grieve for you. There is nothing our friends and family can say or do to take away our pain. Grieving is as individual as we are and it's important to remember that no two people grieve the same. There are no "shoulds" in how to feel, so try not to be too hard on others and give yourself permission to feel whatever you are feeling. It is okay and normal to feel just about any emotion that comes up.

Elizabeth Kubler Ross, a Swiss-born psychiatrist and pioneer on near-death studies, wrote several books on the subject of grief and created the well-known guideline of the five stages of grief. They are: Denial, Anger, Bargaining, Depression and Acceptance. There seems to be a question of whether Kubler Ross's guideline is for the grievers or the ones close to death, but in the context of this book, we will cover them for the grieving.

After you lose a loved one, the last thing you think you will ever feel is acceptance. And honestly, some people never get to the point of feeling like they've accepted their loved one's death, and that's okay. The five stages Kubler Ross outlined are both a guideline to the feelings of grief you may be feeling, and also an example of how to break the process of grief down.

Your feelings may not arise in this order and your emotions are more likely to move around from one stage to another. For example, you could feel anger in the beginning and then it could resurface later, once you've processed some of what happened to your loved one. Not only is there no definite order to grieving, there is no time frame for your feelings to move from one emotion to another. The shifts just happen and move through when they are ready…like waves.

Why do we feel grief? Feelings of grief are the result of loving someone so much that the idea of their physical presence not being with us anymore is so overwhelming and painful that our bodies and minds react this way. In a beautiful way, grief is a testament to our love for the person we lost and our efforts to make a new life without them.

There are a few common themes of grieving. By "common themes" I mean the universal feelings that come up for people: disbelief, sadness, anger, guilt, hopelessness. etc... None of it is welcome or comfortable, but it is all okay and normal.

You really don't need to learn grief. The pain of grief will just come and your body and soul will experience it however you need to experience it. What you do need to learn is how to live with grief — how to experience it and go on living.

Synonyms of grief that may be addressed throughout this book include sorrow, misery, sadness, anguish, pain, distress, heartache, heartbreak, agony, torment, affliction, suffering, woe, desolation, dejection, despair, mourning, mournfulness, bereavement, lamentation. Most of us at one time or another felt one or more of these feelings as it relates to the death of our loved one. Once again, these feelings are normal and expected. They might come in waves of emotion or a stabbing feeling that takes your breath away. Or it might feel like a heaviness that takes over your body and stays there, where moving and breathing is hard to do. We all experience it a little differently and feel it differently in our bodies.

The purpose of this book is to help you learn how to live with grief - how to experience it and understand the pain with some gentle guidance for getting through the worst of it. That's not to say that any of this will be quick or pain-free, and everything obviously can't be covered, but I am sharing what helped me during my worst times, and what I have learned by seeing others through theirs, in hope of helping you.

CHAPTER 2

YOUR HEALTH

Ich habe Kopfschmerzen
Elle a cassé sa jambe
Мы имеем грипп

In every language you learn, you need to know how to describe your physical condition and get medical help when needed. Once you begin speaking Grief, you will need to know how to maintain your own physical health. It is so important to take care of yourself at this stage.

One big issue that comes up when you are grieving is sleep. Sleeping is very important! I can't emphasize this enough. Many people have trouble sleeping before their loved one dies, either because they are sitting up with them, caring for them, or just worrying in general. The stress before a death and after can put your sleep schedule way off. It might not get better for a while after your loved one dies, either.

There's so much to think about, remember and agonize over. It's hard to turn our minds off and let our bodies relax, but it really is vital for everyone's health to get enough sleep.

Talk to your doctor if you need to. If you find yourself awake many nights in a row or tossing and turning repeatedly, that would be a good time to make that call. They might have suggestions for how to sleep better. Meditation or deep breathing will help to relax you too. So will taking a warm shower or bath before bed or having something warm to drink. A friend who works with essential oils says certain oils help with relaxation and sleep as well. Lavender and chamomile are good examples of this.

After my daughter's death, between not being able to breathe from having panic attacks and being used to staying up late with her, I just could not switch my sleep clock. For a few months I would toss and turn until around three a.m. and then finally fall asleep. The things that helped me were to try to wind down earlier than usual by listening to music and focusing on a happy memory I had with my daughter. It also helped to take a warm shower before I got into bed and some television shows that were light and funny used to distract me too. That made it easier for me to settle in at night.

There is no magic cure and you might have to try a few things before you find something that will work for you. And it may not work all the time, but if it works some of the time, or most of the time, then that's pretty good.

Anything you do to let your body rest is helpful for your mind and your health. Napping is another option. Some people don't like the feeling they have when they wake up from a nap, but since you're grieving, getting a small break during the day might be just what you need. Plus, it is a good mental break for you and your body.

If you find you are unable to return to a normal sleep pattern, or maybe you have anxiety related to sleeping, don't wait too long to speak to a doctor or counselor about it. There can be serious medical and mental health consequences from lack of sleep, and it is so important that you live a healthy life after loss.

Even if you are able to sleep, something that comes up with everyone after a loss is the realization as you are first waking up that your loved one is really gone, at least physically. Sometimes that first thought can be like feeling the pain all over again, and it becomes hard to wake up and get out of bed initially. This will get easier over time.

Eating is another issue that comes up when you're grieving. It's common for people to feel sick to their stomachs after their loved one dies or skip food because nothing sounds good to them anymore. Others eat excessively to try to fill the gaping hole that is left inside of them after a loss. It's understandable why food is an issue, but both extremes are harmful to your well-being. It's important to eat to stay as strong and healthy as we can, even if we really don't feel like it. Examine your eating habits following your loss, and if you cannot get yourself to return to a normal, healthy diet, talk to your doctor or another professional.

Grief often brings the same symptoms as depression, including feeling like you are not worthy of taking care of yourself, but I am telling you, there is a reason you are still alive and in this world, and eventually you won't feel this bad. You may not understand it now, but please try to take care of yourself until you do. If you are not going to eat much, finding small healthy meals is a good idea. This might be something your friends and family can provide for you for a little while. Don't feel ashamed to ask. Allowing friends to do something tangible for you makes them feel like they are helping you.

At the opposite end of the spectrum, comfort food is ok but there has to be a limit. It might feel good to eat to fill that void, but if we are trying our best to take care of ourselves, it's best to not overdo it right now. Physical discomfort can also add to your mental stress. I know this is easier said than done, and it is okay to have a day (or two) where you can't control yourself and your eating. But if you are having trouble and one day becomes four or five or more days, then you may need more assistance in processing your grief. There are specialists that can help you with your feelings as it relates to overeating. Be kind to yourself and ask for help if you need it.

Some people try to eat what their loved one liked when they were alive. That's okay too, but if I ate only what my daughter liked I would be eating noodles and chocolate all the time! My daughter's favorite treat was See's Candy, so our family makes it a point to get a few pieces to honor her a couple times a year. We go out on my daughter's birthday and her death day and choose our pieces to remember her. Eating what your loved one liked is a nice way to honor them and it may make you feel closer to them at least for a moment. I have a confession to make...I do still eat at least a little chocolate every day. I do that for me and for her. :)

The emotional toll of grief can affect your physical health in unexpected ways as well. It can be painful and hard to move in the beginning. Right after my daughter died, my heart physically hurt and it felt difficult to breathe. My body seemed to have forgotten how. Someone suggested I get back into yoga, which I had been doing during my pregnancy and for me it was the best thing. I cried in the class a lot but the lights were low and no one even noticed.

It is so important to take care of yourself physically as you go on this journey. Movement helps with all the senses. Starting with something as easy as walking around the block will get you out of the house. One block might turn into several and then you might get to a mile or two or more. Walking on the beach is very soothing if you have a beach near you. There is something about the feel of the sand under your feet and the sound of the ocean that makes you realize how small we are in this vast world, but also how connected we are. Just like with everything else, you need to find what movement will work for you. You have so many options to choose from!

EXERCISE:

As I mentioned in this chapter, taking care of yourself is so important. Find ten minutes a day to try to get outside and find one thing you see that is beautiful. Set a timer if you want to. The weather doesn't matter. Whenever there is sunshine, it is beautiful, but when it is raining, I look towards the sky to see if I can find a break in the clouds so I don't miss seeing a rainbow. It could be raindrops on a leaf or the way the snow falls or the way the sun shines through the clouds or trees. It could even be your dog or cat enjoying outside with you. You can watch them and see the world through their eyes. Once you are outside you may decide to walk a little while. Start with five or ten minutes and do an additional minute every day until you hit 30 or 60 or whatever you can spare. You might find that just getting outside will change your mood for a little while and give you a break from the crushing feelings you are having. And it has the added benefit of being good for your health.

CHAPTER 3

PHYSICAL PRESENCE AND ABSENCE

Je suis ici.
Unsere Freunde sind dort.
Ella esta no más con nosotros.

When learning any new language, one of the earliest lessons is how to describe the physical presence of people. "I am here." "Our friends are over there." "She is no longer with us." In the language of Grief, you have to learn how to process the physical absence of someone who has been such a significant part of your life.

In my opinion one of the hardest things to cope with after a loss is missing someone's physical body. Even if we believe our loved one is still around us, the fact that we can't see, touch or have back and forth interactions with them makes our loss that much harder.

If your loved one died away from home, coming home without them for the first time will most probably be shocking and painful for you and your family. The first time I walked into our house without my daughter I could immediately feel the huge void her absence left us with. In a way the house felt hollow and empty, and at the same time it felt like she was everywhere and in everything. I cried and cried as I went into every room and that feeling of emptiness settled in. It took a while for that feeling to go away every time I came home.

When someone dies at home there is a similar feeling of that huge void, but there is an additional feeling of dread when an outsider finally needs to remove the body of your loved one. That dread comes from not only losing that physical person, but also dreading the emptiness that will be left.

If your loved one died in the living room or the bedroom or anywhere else, there is almost the feeling of a hollow void that is left. It's normal to feel sad or strange when entering the room they died in. It could feel creepy or scary at first, but eventually it can feel comforting that your loved one's essence might still be in the house. I've had friends who wanted to snuggle up right where their loved one was laying before they died. Others didn't even want to be in the same room for a long time. You need to decide what is right for you, and whatever you decide is fine. It is part of your healing process.

Depending on the area you live, you could stay with the body of your loved one after they die. The George Mark House in northern California, which is the first freestanding pediatric palliative care facility, actually has a room with a cooling bed in it so the family can stay with the body as long as they need to. For some, being with the body of their loved one is helpful in processing the death. Others feel it is weird or gives them an uneasy feeling. Again, there is no right or wrong here, so try to reserve judgment on others and don't allow anyone to put theirs on you.

Having a body taken from your home or leaving your loved one at the hospital or hospice can bring dread and be a traumatic experience. When the body is actually taken away from your home it can be very difficult. The coroner or funeral home will carry the body out or put it in a bag first, which can be really awful for the family left behind. Some people want to stay with the body as long as they can and some choose to go in the other room because it's just too hard to see what's happening. If hospice has been involved they can be helpful with the support needed for the removal as well. Once the body is gone, that void creeps in. It is normal and okay to feel strange, uneasy and sad in that spot. I promise this feeling won't last forever. It just takes some getting used to.

The same feeling of dread may be present if someone died in the hospital and you had to leave without them. Saying goodbye to that physical part of someone is overwhelming and painful and it feels so permanent. Having the support of other family members, friends or even nurses and clergy can be helpful in getting you through the initial shock of losing someone. It can be a paralyzing and overwhelming experience, and it's okay to reach out to others to help get you through.

Write down the questions you might have while you have them on your mind regarding the process. It might be hard to remember on your own all the questions you want to ask, since death can feel shocking, especially in the beginning. Depending on where you live and what the role is of the medical staff involved, you might be able to get the support you need from them.

If someone has been sick for a while and in the hospital, you may be assigned a social worker. They can be very helpful in guiding you through, and don't be afraid to take advantage of this assistance. If you have supportive family and friends, they can do the asking for you if that helps you. You might also need someone to drive you home, since you will probably be in no shape to do that yourself. Don't be afraid to speak up and communicate your needs. Take care of yourself.

Other scenarios you might find yourself in are finding out about a death while you are away from home. There can be many scenarios in this case. If you have a college student, there is an online support group for kids who are away at school when their parent or other family member dies. If you are away from home when someone dies, some airlines offer grief fares in most cases. You will need to ask what each company offers. For any circumstance, this is a really difficult time and everyone understands that.

Decisions

When someone dies, there are suddenly questions to be answered and dozens of decisions that need to be made that you may never have discussed or even contemplated. Your support system can help you with decisions regarding the funeral or burial arrangements, as those generally top the list. Hopefully your loved one had written down their wishes for after their death, but if they didn't and you need to make these decisions, or it was a younger person who would not have discussed their death with you, then it can be incredibly painful and difficult.

You may feel like you are in no position to make big decisions like these, so don't be afraid to ask for help. If you don't have someone close to you to help, maybe a nurse from the hospital or the hospice worker who was at the home and got to know your loved one, or a religious leader who knows you and your family can give some assistance.

Don't make decisions too quickly or without thinking them all the way through, but also, give yourself the freedom to get some things wrong and move on. No one is perfect, especially not in moments of grief.

My daughter loved Mickey and Minnie Mouse and she had little stuffed ones that she carried around with her everywhere. They were given to her by a special babysitter, and when she died, we made the decision to bury my daughter with those dolls because she loved them so much. At the time I thought it was the right thing to do. In my mind I had hoped the dolls would give my daughter comfort as she moved on, but a few years after she died I was heartbroken because I realized I wanted those dolls! I felt I really needed them! They would have comforted me and made me feel closer to my daughter, especially as time was marching on. I wished I had kept Mickey and Minnie and they didn't get buried with her, but it was too late for us to change our minds. As a result, I had to learn to accept the decision, forgive myself, and move on.

It is very common for people to bury their loved ones with items that meant a lot to them while they were alive. It is a lovely idea and one that can be meaningful for the family, knowing your loved one will take this item with them on their journey beyond this life. Not everyone will regret sending an item with them and for your family this might be a non-issue. On the other hand it might be a discussion you and your family want to think carefully about before the burial or cremation.

There is no right or wrong answer here. You have to go with your heart and decide what feels best for you at the time. I know there is so much to think about and this is one more thing, so please don't stress yourself out about this! Do what you think is best. Whatever you decide is okay. This was just my experience and something I wanted to share.

Practical considerations — what to do with their "stuff"

Sometimes, after a death, we need to deal with the person's belongings. They might have lived in your house and going in their room will be very hard initially. Maybe they had their own home and you are in charge of going through their items, which can be very difficult and emotional. There is an unspoken rule about going through your loved one's things, that I have gleaned from conversations with many grieving people: it's better not to get rid of any items for one year.

If you need to clear out an apartment or a house, then box their things up and give yourself time to look at the items and go through them when you're ready. If your loved one lived in your home and going in their room is painful, then leave their room alone. Some people leave their loved one's room the way it was for years. That's okay if that works for you. Some people like to build a shrine for the person who died. If that makes you feel better, then do it. Just make sure everyone in the home is okay with it. If someone isn't, have an honest, open conversation about everyone's needs in this regard.

Don't let your friends or family tell you that you should throw any items away or get rid of things. You have to do this on your time and when you're ready. If there is a need to dispose of things quickly, then that's okay, but I know many people who had regrets later for items they wished they would have held onto. For example, I worked with a man whose wife died of breast cancer several years ago. He was so heartbroken about her death that seeing his wife's things in their house only seemed to make him feel worse.

His two daughters were away at school and he decided before they came home the next time that he would pack her stuff up and take it all to the local Goodwill. A few things happened after this. Once everything was out of the house he had an incredible amount of guilt about clearing his wife's items out. He also realized that even though it was hard to look at her things, having all of it gone felt as if she never existed in his life. He had even taken down their pictures!

The other thing that happened was his daughters were furious with him. He had kept a few items of jewelry, but that was it. One of his daughters tearfully said to me later, "He never thought about if I wanted to wear my mom's pajamas or even a sweatshirt to make me feel closer to her. I am heartbroken he gave everything away!" Luckily he had put all the pictures in a box so his daughters were relieved at least they had those memories, but both were sad and angry that this decision was made without them.

This is similar to an experience I had and one that has stuck with me, even after all this time. A day or two after my daughter died, my mom and my sister-in-law decided to wash all my daughter's clothes and linens from her bed.

It was a gesture that was meant to be helpful, but I can tell you, the smell of my daughter was washed away from everything! I was devastated!

So even if you think washing everything and putting it away or throwing it out is the best option, you might want to consider waiting a little while. You could find that your loved one's scent is on something and it will be a comfort to hold onto for a while. Eventually the scent will go away on its own, but this is something to be aware of and something that is not really ever talked about.

Getting through those first few days...and the days after that

My daughter's funeral was on a bright and sunny day. I remember thinking right after the ceremony, "How can the sun be shining? Doesn't everyone know I just had to bury my daughter?" How could life just be moving on? It didn't seem fair that people were laughing and going on with their lives when I was in so much pain. Unfortunately, this is a part of life and one of the many things we have no control over. Life will go on, whether we think it should or not.

After the funeral and the initial chaos, and after the visitors start coming less and less, there will be a period where the silence feels deafening. There are many people that have no support and no family and they are really alone in this process. Others have a nice support system where family and friends might check in with them well after their loved one has died. Either way, it is a difficult time for everyone when things calm down and the reality of the situation starts to settle in. You finally have the quiet that puts you back in your head with the painful memories and conversations.

This is where our bodies try to protect us, and being numb can sometimes be helpful, but it is still an incredibly difficult time of adjustment. This is also where different people might need different things in this process. One person might want to be left alone and another might need to take a walk and talk their feelings out. Someone might cry all the time while someone else is so angry they feel like they want to put their fist through a wall. Other people might have the need to work out or take a road trip or scream at the top of their lungs to release some of those pent up feelings, while others might want to be creative and write or paint or scrapbook.

It is all okay!

You have to decide for you what will make you feel a sliver better for a moment and do that, so long as it doesn't hurt you or anyone else.

As time continues you will need brief periods of relief from your sadness and heartache. For me, after the first month, yoga and scrapbooking gave me something to focus on and helped me get through my worst days. For my husband it was working out in the gym and running.

Grief takes up so much energy and focus in our lives that we need to give our minds and our bodies a break. Any break we can get is a relief because living with grief is exhausting!

EXERCISE:

Come up with one activity that makes you feel better about being alive. It could be something you have always liked to do, or maybe there is something you used to do with your loved one. Write it down. Give yourself permission to do it. Find a way to fit it into your day and allow yourself to feel relief from your grief when you're doing it.

If nothing sounds interesting right now, then try something anyway. Anything that could be a small distraction will be helpful. If the thing you try doesn't sit well with you, then try something else. If you don't have the energy to choose something, then maybe a close friend or family member can help you with this. This idea of finding something creative is not going to take away from the pain you are feeling. It is just one more tool to help you get through the worst of it.

When the Real World comes to get you

Often, even if people are still grieving and feeling like they are not ready to be thrown into the real world, real life demands (kids, school, work) might be something you are forced to deal with before you are ready. This could be either because you have always been the provider for your family or you have had to become financially responsible due to the death of your loved one. Some places of work are more forgiving if you need more time for yourself, but some have very strict rules about taking time off, even if it is for a loved one's death.

It's a luxury if you don't need to work and you can focus on getting through your grief, but for most people that is not the case. I was lucky enough to not have to work after my daughter died, but my husband was responsible for us financially and forced himself to go back right away. At the time, he owned his own business with two partners and he needed to be there. He said he was able to compartmentalize his grief to get through the days, but there were also times when he had to close his office door to try to gather himself and his emotions. He also gave himself time in the car to cry and grieve on the way to work and back home. I guess for him it was lucky that he had such a long commute.

My hope for you is that your place of business gives you some time off and is also patient with your feelings and emotions. You could have ups and downs for a while and it helps if you have support from your workplace. Take it one day at a time and do the best you can, and if you need to cry, then cry. If you are not allowed to cry at your desk, then the bathroom or right outside might be where you can let it out.

Stress in the workplace can be overwhelming after a loss. It is important to have tools to help you if you feel you need it. In her book, "Happiness as a Second Language," there's a chapter on dealing with negative people in which Valerie Alexander talks about creating an energy shield when someone says something to you that might put you in a negative spiral or upset you. When you are grieving, the smallest thing can set you crying, but if you have to keep it together and your boss, for example, is not the most sympathetic person, then try to imagine there is actually a thick glass wall that is going up around you and protecting you. You still might be sad, but putting up the imaginary wall can protect you from outside negativity. Imagine the insensitive words from a coworker or boss just bouncing off the wall and bouncing away from you.

You can also imagine your loved one wrapping themselves around you and shielding you from whatever words might be upsetting you. People can be very inconsiderate and oblivious at times, so hang in there. The first few months are rough! After a while you might get used to your work environment, or you may find that you need a change to fit the changes going on in your life. Proceed with caution though. It's never a good idea to make major life decisions

– like quitting your job – while grieving. See instead if you can take a leave of absence or a medical leave to care for your own well-being. Do what's best for you, both to get through these initial days and in the long run.

Another thing that might be helpful at some point down the road is to volunteer your time with an organization that is meaningful for you or the loved one you lost. I am not talking about doing this immediately. Although some people want to get involved with something right away, it is not for everyone. About six months after our daughter died, my husband and I started going to a grief support group (TCF–The Compassionate Friends) for people who have lost a child. After several years of going to this group once a month, we began to facilitate our local chapter's meeting. Seven years after my daughter's death, we were asked to be the Co-chairs of TCF's National Conference taking place in Hollywood, California that year.

It was a tremendous amount of work, but it turned out to be such an amazing and meaningful experience. And we got to do it all in memory of our daughter, which made it worth all the work and effort we put in. There are organizations for everything and they all could use your help. If your loved one was killed by a drunk driver or had cancer or was murdered, find a group that addresses that issue. It will be beneficial for you, too, meeting other people who has had a similar experience with losing their loved one.

Start off small and see if getting involved might be right for you. It always feels good to give back. The organization you find will be grateful for your help and you can do the work in memory of your loved one. Every story is different, but there are always parts of someone's story you can relate to, or maybe the feelings that come up feel similar to someone else's and you may make a connection with that person. Also the Internet is a wealth of information on this subject, so when you're ready, start there.

CHAPTER 4

Family

Mi Madre
您的姐妹
τα παιδιά μας

Do you remember studying a foreign language and learning all the family words? Mother, father, brother, aunt, cousin, grandmother, children. There are many definitions of family. Today, those definitions have expanded far beyond the traditional ones. The traditional definition is, "A group consisting of two parents and children living together as a unit."

Your family could fit this description or maybe it's very different from that. The Urban Dictionary's definition is, "A group of people, usually of the same bloodline (but they don't have to be), who genuinely love, trust, care about and look out for each other." I am lucky enough to have a close family, and my family and my husband's family get along, so that makes things so much easier.

Both the makeup and dynamics are different in every family. When someone dies, we all hope that our family and friends will love and support us through our grieving, but that is not always the case. Sometimes loss does bring people together, but other times the stress of grieving and the details that go with it can tear families apart. People sometimes lose sight of why the family is together and bad feelings can erupt.

Family is so important. Maybe your family is a little crazy and dysfunctional and your friends are your family. That's okay too. But remember, it's easier to get through loss with some support, and hopefully your family can do that for you.

I have two different friends who don't talk to their siblings anymore since the death of both their parents. In both cases there were issues that came up as they were trying to settle their parents' estates. In every situation, there will be inevitable differences of opinion on how to solve any number of issues. You may not see eye-to-eye with other people in your family, especially if there is not a will or directive left behind. But hopefully the mutual love of your loved one and each other will help keep things in perspective for everyone involved. Compromise can almost always be achieved or outside guidance might be needed for the sake of family peace.

One suggestion for how to communicate when things are stressful and no one is in agreement is to have everyone write down their concerns and what they hope to get out of this experience emotionally and materially. Maybe there was a special piece of jewelry that one person might want or something that has meaning for different family members that can be divided up. It would be good to have a mediator at this point who is not emotionally involved. That could be a friend of the family or someone you hire. That way everyone's thoughts can be voiced and hopefully a peaceful resolution can be found, as well as a way to support each other.

But many people have family members who are unreasonable and impossible. And many family members stay close hoping just to get money, if there is any. It may be that there is no way there can be a resolution because of the personalities involved. You can only try to keep the lines of communication open, but you can't force someone to feel the way you do or act in a way you would deem appropriate in this environment.

If your end goal is to have a relationship with your other family members despite your differences, then be conscious of keeping your anger in check when you speak, and try to talk to them while you are calm and feeling stronger. At this time, if you are able, it would be very helpful to have a bereavement therapist to help navigate the family dynamics and work towards a resolution that works for everyone. They are trained to be able to work with all kinds of situations and circumstances and having an outside person can sometimes be helpful.

Everyone has to agree to get together of course. That might be half the battle, but once everyone is there, the bereavement therapist will help your family to let go of resentments that may be involved and help work through the issues your family is stuck in. If a little time has passed, that is still okay. Sometimes leaving an issue alone for a short time can be helpful because when you revisit it, you might not feel as upset or angry. If it's easier to write down your feelings and needs before you go into a session, that might be helpful to keep your thoughts in order. If there is one family member that you are closest to, another idea is to reach out to them first to start the process. Then when you all finally get together you won't feel as alone. Just make sure no one else feels that the two of you are working as a team or ganging up on them.

You still can't control how others feel or respond, but if you've said everything you want to, then you have to leave it alone and hope they will be reasonable in their response. If the relationship means enough to you, then it would be important to continue to try, at least for a while. It may be things are too emotional now, but in the future; three months, six months or a year down the line, it might be a good idea to keep the lines of communication open in case feelings have changed and you can work out an agreement. Even if it's been five, ten or twenty years since the loss of your loved one that caused the rift, the door to your surviving family members does not have to be permanently shut. Try some of the options I laid out above to open the lines of communication. The rewards might be enormous.

There are always situations where no resolution can happen. That is very sad, but it is not uncommon. If you need to walk away for your own self-preservation, then do what you have to do. It always helped me to realize that certain people just don't have the capacity to do any better than they are doing. Whatever your situation is, try to make sure YOU have the support you need to get through the day of the funeral and the upcoming difficult weeks and months. This whole time can be very stressful and difficult for everyone involved.

It is also important to remember that you are not the only one that had a loss. If the person who died is your child or your parent, you may feel it harder than anyone else, but you can't really measure pain and it would not be fair to tell someone in your family that you are hurting more than they are. Everyone grieves in their own way and shows it differently. Just try to be aware as you go through this journey that the loss in your family has affected not only you and the immediate family members, but extended family and friends as well.

When my daughter died, my niece and nephew were still in elementary school. I was not in any shape to be worried about anyone else's emotional state at the time, but I found out later how hard my daughter's death was on them. Years later my nephew had written a school report about my daughter that really touched me, and my niece now has a tattoo of my daughter's name on her body. I could not have supported them initially, but I just didn't realize the effect my daughter's life had on everyone else in our family.

Grief and Children

An important consideration in this process are the young family members who might be grieving along with you. It's hard to imagine trying to support anyone else while you feel so awful but that is a real possibility. If you are a parent and your parent, grandparent or spouse died, or maybe you lost a child and your children lost a sibling, they will need their own support, and they will need much of it from you.

Depending on the age of the child, they process death differently than adults do. As adults we kind of live and breathe grief all the time. It becomes hard to set it aside. Kids don't do that. They are very good at compartmentalizing their feelings. They may or may not want to talk about their feelings with you and from the outside they could look like they are just fine. But they, like us, are trying desperately to understand and process what has happened. They could also be frightened by seeing all the adults around them upset and things not going on as normal.

Younger kids are more apt to open up about their feelings if they are playing or distracted. One suggestion would be to color with them, play ball or build something. Hopefully this will make it easier for them to open up to you. From my experience, it is easier for kids to express themselves if they are doing something active. They won't want to be sitting in a room and talking about their feelings with you. They will always be less likely to open up that way. In most cities there are support groups for kids who have lost someone, or there may be a special teacher or therapist who can work with your child if you need additional help with how to deal with their feelings.

A common thought that comes up with kids after a close death is the fear that another family member will die too. For example, if a child loses a parent, it is very normal for them to fear losing their other parent as well. All we can really do is assure them we will try our best to stay with them always. None of us know what our future holds, but just make sure your kids know that you love them and if you had a choice you would stay with them forever.

It is also okay to cry in front of your child. Try to explain, if you can, why you are crying and why you feel sad. It will also give them permission to share their feelings with you. If you are crying, you have to remember your kids are not there to comfort you. You still need to assure them that you will be okay and it is also okay to be sad. It puts an incredible burden on them if they feel like they need to comfort you and make you feel better. Don't be afraid to show them your feelings and explain that though sad now, things will be different, but ok again, even if you don't quite believe it yet.

Many years after my daughter died, I volunteered with an amazing organization in the Los Angeles area called Our House. They have all kinds of grief support for different losses. When I worked with them, I worked with a group of four-to-seven year old kids who had lost a parent. In our group we did all kinds of games and art projects with the kids to try to make them comfortable to talk about the parent who died. Most of the time it was fun with a little serious mixed in, and the kids almost never cried or got emotional.

But once in a while we would have a serious session and it would be heartbreaking to see how the kids were struggling with trying to understand why their parent had to go away.

After my daughter died, I had two more children. I wanted them to know about her and started talking about her with them when they were still babies. As they got older, they asked me questions even from a very young age about what happened to their sister. Their questions got more thoughtful as the years went on and they tried to understand.

As kids' brains develop, they are able to understand more, and as time goes by, it would be nice for them to be able to come to you and ask questions about the person who died. They are trying to understand and process just like you. It is so important to include them and be open with them. They understand more than we give them credit for and they can feel all the emotions in the house anyway.

Sometimes the questions they ask are hard to answer and it's okay to tell your child you don't know, or turn around and ask them what they think about a particular subject. For example. "Where do you think your grandma is?" or "I wonder what they're doing, too. What do you think they're doing?"

Kids can have amazing and profound answers when you let them express themselves. The more honest you are with your kids the better, but make sure they are developmentally ready to hear what you're talking about. If the loss was a violent one or disturbing in any way, it would be very important to wait to give the child details like that until they are older. Maybe you can give them bits of information at a time and as they grow up and develop they can hear more details little by little.

Teenagers react differently as well. Generally they will not want to talk about your loved one to you for fear of getting you upset. They don't like to see you upset and they won't want you to see them upset either. Try not to push them. Older kids need to be with their peers or other kids that have gone through a similar experience. They may seem more angry than sad because they are also trying to process this enormous loss. Try to give them time and space and be sensitive if they decide they want to talk. It is hard enough being a teenager without having to deal with all the emotions that go with losing a loved one.

Some families don't believe in including children in what's going on if their loved one is very sick at home or in the hospital. Once they have died, the kids are sometimes not included in the funeral and the discussions that follow. A lot of families believe this is a way to protect their kids. The opposite is actually true.

Kids can process better if they know the whole story. If their parent went in the hospital one week and never came home, the child will have so many questions about why they didn't come home. They will also be afraid of hospitals. If they are not allowed to see their loved one before they die, they'll be confused about what happened and feel very left out and sad. For little kids it's okay to tell them that their loved one doesn't feel well and that their body is not working very well right now. Then when they see their loved one, explain what is going on with them. Maybe they are on oxygen or are unconscious. It will be scary for a child if you don't explain what is happening and why. Remember, you need to explain to them, keeping in mind their age. Even though many questions will follow, it really is not fair to leave them out.

When they were young, I explained to my own kids, when they asked, that everyone has a heart and we need our heart to pump in order for our bodies to stay alive. Their sister's heart didn't work right after she was born so it stopped and she died. They understood that and over the years would just ask me out of the blue, "So, when your heart stops, you die, right?" I would tell them they were correct and they would move on to the next subject. When their elementary school classes started talking about the body each of them told their teacher that they had a sister who died because her heart stopped working. Of course then the teacher would contact me to report they had an interesting conversation with my child. I assured the teachers they were accurate. My kids were always very matter-of-fact about what had happened because I was always open with them and tried to explain so they could understand. For our family, this worked.

Give your kids the opportunity to say goodbye to their loved one if you can. It will help in their grieving process. Also try not to tell them their loved one was very sick because the next time someone gets the flu, kids can become very fearful for that person or themselves. It's easier for them to understand if you say their body wasn't working right or there was something wrong with the inside of their body. If the death involved mental illness, it is okay to tell your kids there was something unhealthy about their loved one's brain. You might be surprised how well your kids handle this situation. There is always outside help with a therapist or a school counselor if you need additional guidance trying to decide what to tell your children and how to tell them.

EXERCISE:

If you have a young child in your home who is also dealing with a loss, draw a picture together. Ask them about your loved one and either have them draw their best memory of them together or maybe where they think their loved one is now. You could try to make your own picture too. While you are coloring you might be able to get your child to open up about how they are feeling and what has been hard for them. Don't push them but see if they will share any of their feelings with you. It can be a good bonding experience and you will know better how to support them.

For older kids, maybe suggest taking a walk or a hike. Playing ball is another option, or suggest shopping or something your child likes to do. Some kids will be more talkative if they are looking in stores or doing something busy. You know your child best, so do what works for both of you.

CHAPTER 5

TIME AND SIGNS

Quando è?
È in punto di 7:00.

Learning how to tell time in a new language is usually basic and fairly easy. Learning how to tell time in the language of Grief is far more complex.

When your loved one dies, time seems to slow down. Way down! It feels slow and thick, like you're moving through molasses. In the beginning, right after my daughter died, I calculated the hours she had been gone and then the days and months. I even looked at the time and calculated, "twenty four hours ago at this time, this happened" or "at 6:00 pm on Monday a week ago, that happened." It was hard not to think of what had been happening the day before or month before at that time.

With the passing of time came the feeling of dread that my daughter had been gone longer and longer from me. And yet, time still marched on. But all I wanted was for it to stop and go backwards! She would miss so much and I would miss her doing so many things. I wasn't sure in the beginning if I would ever get over that. There was always this glaring void with her gone. That feeling of being aware of time, all the time, is perfectly normal as it relates to grief and it takes a while to get over, but it does get better eventually.

Special dates like the person's birthday or the day they died also become important and difficult days for most people. I will talk later in the book about possible ideas for getting through birthdays and death days. Holidays and other celebrations also are a reminder that the absence of the person we love is so obvious and empty. For years, my husband and I went to the beach on my daughter's birthday and death day. Something about being near the water, with the feeling of the sand under my feet helped me connect with the earth, which in turn made me feel closer to my daughter.

In the beginning it's hard to remember all the good times we shared with the person who died. People tend to go over the way they died or the last conversation they had with that person. A lot of times it's like a running tape in your head. I have talked to people who were up at night for weeks after a death and their minds wouldn't or couldn't shut off. Other people go to work and they can't concentrate or they become absent minded.

A woman in our community had a father who was an avid mountain climber. As he accomplished some of the big mountains close by, he decided on his big birthday to try to tackle the harder ones farther away. He had flown with a few friends to the Far East to climb one of the most difficult mountains, but much to his family's horror, he was in a freak accident and fell to his death.

When I spoke to the family a few months after the accident, all any of them could think about was the fight they had before he left, when they had begged him not to go on the trip. They had all said some strong words to each other, and each one in the family kept picturing what the accident might have looked like and wondered if he suffered. There was sadness, anger and guilt over what had been said, and his daughter recalled to me, "It's as if I am stuck in this bubble and I can only see this last week of his life. This painful horrible week! But he had an amazing life, even though it was cut short. And so many people loved him!"

There is no easy way to get through the slowing of time except to know that it won't always feel this way. I promise! The initial shock of losing a loved one, even if you expect it, is so jarring on your body and soul, it puts everything off: time, your body, and your sense of what is right in the world.

It takes different amounts of time for everyone to feel more normal, to feel like moving on is a possibility. I don't mean moving on and "getting over it." I mean actually moving forward in your life, so that time feels more normal and not so stuck. Please know the feeling of slowed time is part of the process of grief and it will change. Over time.

For me, it was at the beginning of grief, the first month or two or three that felt harder and more difficult to get through as it relates to time. Depending on the person or the circumstance, you could feel this feeling for less time or much more, but however long it feels this way, this is all perfectly normal.

Signs

For some reason, numbers become extremely important when someone close to you dies. In grief, the bereaved can find themselves obsessing over them. This is also normal and perfectly fine, especially in the early days following a loss.

My daughter died on March 23rd. It seemed those first few weeks that every time I looked at the clock it was 3:23 (or 11:23 or 8:23). It was really strange. Those numbers still come up a lot, even now, and it always reminds me of my daughter, but now when I see it, I feel comforted.

Recently, when I look at the clock the time always seems to be 11:11 or 2:22 or 4:44. I'm not sure what that means, and it probably means nothing, but I am aware that it's happening all the time lately, and it gives me a moment to pause and be mindful.

Certain numbers become very important to people. It could be the day of your loved one's birthday or their death day. Many people create rituals on those days to help them get through them. We will talk about that later in the book. It could also be the age that your loved one was when they passed. People find other things, too, that can remind them of their loved one.

My mom started finding two pennies everywhere she went and since my daughter was two when she died, it made my mom feel like she was closer to her. She would call me and tell me every time two pennies crossed her path. A lot of people I have met say that they have found money or things in their path that they associated with their loved one. It could be change, a flower or a feather, rocks or shells. It could also be items in the shape of hearts or wings or something else.

I have talked to countless people who said there were times or dates that were important to them surrounding their loved one's death. Or they had special dates and numbers that reminded them of their loved one whenever they came upon them. Sometimes they came across items that made them feel like their loved one put that in their path. I have heard all kinds of crazy coincidences...that maybe aren't just coincidences, but the energy of our loved ones staying with us somehow.

Those numbers will always be a sensitive issue and meaningful for you, and that is perfectly okay. It's kind of nice to take some of the things we see or come across as a sign from our loved ones. We might not know for sure what these little signs mean, but it does make us feel better and closer to them in that moment.

Another thing that seems to happen often is animal and insect sightings. A lot of people associate butterflies or dragonflies with their departed loved one. Another friend used to see hummingbirds whenever she thought of her grandmother.

It might be in an unusual place and you will see your unique creatures hovering around or circling above you. You could also see it in a magazine or on TV. Be aware whenever you see something that makes you think of your loved one, especially if you see it repeatedly. It could be a small sign for you, if you believe in that.

A dear friend who also lost a child several years ago used to bring her daughter to swim with the dolphins when she was alive. Now, when she is near the water and sees dolphins, it's very meaningful for her and makes her feel like her daughter is close by. There was a cat in our neighborhood that my daughter used to love. She used to talk about that cat constantly. After her death, the cat perched itself in our backyard and stayed around our house for days. It never left. Then once it finally left, the cat would show up once in a while and hang around us, circling our legs. I always felt that maybe it was a sign my daughter was close by. It made me feel good.

Some people are very connected to animals. I took a women's spirituality class from an amazing teacher who I felt very close to. She was my life-line at one point and I ended up going to her classes for years. Once in a while, I met her for a one-on-one appointment and I learned so much from her wisdom.

She had studied with Native Americans and learned many things that she taught to our class, including being more present in our lives and connecting with nature. She taught us that animal sightings and other things that happened to us were important signs to pay attention to. After any bird or other animal would cross our paths, our class would come in and ask her what it meant. She always had amazing reasons why we saw the particular creature when we did and what it meant for our lives, and it was always comforting and so accurate to what was going on in our lives.

She also believed animals give us spiritual messages sometimes. I am always grateful and relieved when I see a butterfly or certain animals in my path. I try to pay attention in case it might mean something for me. Sometimes I can figure out the meaning of a sighting myself, depending on what is going on in my life. Other times I can't see a connection at all. It is always nice when we receive an obvious sign and we don't need to figure anything complicated out about its meaning. For me, seeing butterflies always makes me feel closer to my daughter and I like to believe she is trying to give me a personal sign too, reminding me she is close by.

The family mentioned above who lost their father to a freak mountain climbing accident told me that a blue jay started coming around the kitchen window every day after their father's death. On the fifth day, one of the daughter's wondered out loud to the family if the bird was a sign that their dad was still close by. Or maybe he was the bird! That helped them stop dwelling so much on his death, and opened the door for forward progress.

Going over a loved one's death in our heads the way we tend to is a way for our minds and bodies to grapple with the enormity of our loss. Over time the emotions around the details of the death will not feel as painful or sad, but it takes a long, long time. Go over it as long as you need to in order to process the loss for yourself. And if it helps, track it. Get it down on paper. Give yourself the freedom to pay attention to the thoughts and signs you may be experiencing.

When I was scrapbooking my daughter's life and writing about her, I realized that I was getting signs a lot. I began this exact act of tracking them and writing them down. I mentioned earlier the clock always showing me the number 23. One day that happened six times! Another example was the cat hanging out in our yard. I was trying to notice if I was thinking of my daughter and the cat appeared or if it appeared and that reminded me of my daughter. Either way, paying close attention to those signs helped me process my loss, and made time stop feeling like it was standing still.

EXERCISE:

Keep a notebook and pen handy and write your experiences down. Even if you don't believe in signs, journaling in this way will help you remember the unexplained things that might be happening around you. Write it down and you might be surprised at a pattern or theme that comes up. You never know!

If you don't believe in signs, every day you can still write down one really cool thing that happened that you want to remember, that might make you feel more normal again. After a while, read what you've written. See how present you are in your own life, and how much progress you're making processing your loss, and reaching your new normal.

CHAPTER 6
THE NOUNS OF GRIEF

Catharsis
Expectation

When I think of a noun, I remember what our teachers taught us in grade school. A noun is a person, place or thing. The person, of course, is our loved one. Place and thing can be any number of nouns – where they died, where we first met them, their favorite shirt, that toy they never picked up that made us crazy but that we wish terribly we could trip over just one more time. In the language of Grief, the nouns are the things you need to get you through each day. Those tangible "objects" that help you to process everything that's happening right now.

Catharsis

An important noun to discuss as it relates to grief is Catharsis: the process of releasing, and thereby achieving relief from strong or repressed emotions. It also means purification or cleansing. Grief can feel dense and heavy. As you go through the emotions you are having after a loss and releasing them slowly, there eventually will be some relief of the pain you are feeling, but it takes time for the heaviness to begin to lift. It could take a few months to a few years and there really is no time frame. As you process different aspects of your grief, you will notice a shift and a little lightening of the burdens you might be feeling.

Most definitions emphasize two essential components of Catharsis: Emotional and Cognitive.

Emotional catharsis feels like an "explosive release of deeply troubled, deep rooted, states of suffering within us." One psychiatrist on lovehealth.org described catharsis as an involuntary, instinctive body process. For example, crying, screaming, shaking…that sort of thing. On the opposite end could be spontaneous belly laughter. That sometimes happens as another way for our bodies to get out extreme emotion and it can feel so much better than crying and rage. Your emotions can sometimes feel a little manic at times after a loss and that is actually normal and very common.

The cognitive aspects of catharsis are defined as, "insight, new realization and the unconscious becoming conscious." Also "any extreme change in emotion that results in renewal and restoration." Catharsis isn't something that is felt and then is over. It most probably will be an ongoing thing to release all the pent up emotions you are feeling so you can continue to live with less pain emotionally and cognitively. These moments help, like baby steps, and add up to keep you moving forward.

This will be an exhausting process, so don't be alarmed and don't forget to rest. It can take a lot out of you, both mentally and physically. By giving suggestions and exercises throughout the book, I hope to help you release some of the pain that you are feeling during this process. There is no easy fix with grief, but I can tell you that the pain does lessen and you won't always feel the way you do right now.

Expectation

Another noun that has a critical impact on your grief is Expectation. I'm talking about the expectation we put on ourselves after a death and also the ones our friends and family put on us. It's hard to imagine how we will feel when someone we love dies until it actually happens. If our loved one was sick, we might have imagined how we were going to feel after their death, but in truth, until they die we have no way of knowing the depth of our feelings and emotions.

Three close friends of mine who experienced a more prolonged death with their loved ones were surprised after they died how the pain of grief took over their lives. I think their expectation was that they were going to be prepared for the deaths. Of course they would be sad, but they all thought they were in control of their feelings and felt they knew what to expect. In truth that was not the case with any of them and it is not usually the case with anyone.

Whether your loved one died unexpectedly or if the death was expected, it makes no difference. It's all hard. Every person I have talked to, no matter what the circumstances regarding their loved one's death, said they found the process of grief much harder and more painful than they expected.

I remember after my daughter died, it was getting close to the one-year anniversary of her death. Hitting the one-year mark was a very difficult time for me since it was hard to believe a whole year had gone by without her. Also I didn't feel as numb and so the pain inside me was excruciating. A friend I was close to asked me if I was feeling better and did I feel like I was over my grief. I was stunned and speechless! She obviously had not had a death close to her and so she had no idea what I was really going through.

Her expectation was just one more aspect of grief I was not prepared to deal with.

I also think the expectation of our society is that after a year we should be all healed and over our pain. I'm not sure who came up with that timeline but it is way off! We need to reteach our communities and our society about the length of time it could take to feel more normal again after a loss. In my opinion the timeline on feeling better should be two to twenty years. To those of us who have suffered a loss, that sounds a lot more accurate.

I have found in this situation that it works best to be honest with people about how you are feeling and what you need. This is very important. Your friends and family really won't know what to do for you unless they've been through a loss themselves. It might not feel comfortable to speak up, but that's the only way any of the people close to you will know how to help you. And try not to let their expectations of you force you to do anything you're not ready for. It is perfectly okay to thank someone for their opinion and do what you need to for yourself. Or tell them that you are not ready to do what they think you should be doing, like go out with friends or clean out your loved one's room.

As far as putting expectations on yourself, remember, this is new territory for you and since losing a loved one can change everything, be kind and accepting of yourself and what you might need to get through this. You deserve a break and forgiveness for not knowing how to move forward during this difficult time. Not only is it important to be kind to yourself and give yourself a break, be kind to your friends and family too. It really is impossible for them to always know what we need. Also it is good to keep in mind they do have your best interests at heart.

Bonus Noun — Soul

One other noun that I want to talk about is the Soul, generally defined as, "the spiritual or immaterial part of a human being or animal regarded as immortal." People have differing feelings and beliefs about whether or not there is a part of us that survives death. The main religions tell us our souls return to God or go to heaven after we die, or come back in the body of another creature or person. But when someone dies, it's hard to believe any part of them lives, since their physical body is what we can feel and see and it's no longer with us.

Some people get a lot of comfort in knowing and believing their loved one is still around and some people think this idea is crazy. Whatever you decide for yourself or believe is fine.

There have been ongoing discussions throughout history of whether it matters if the person who died was a good or bad person, and does that determine their fate once they die? Do only good souls go with God to heaven? Is there such thing as Hell? Does God really punish or reward us? Do you even believe in God? These questions are ones that are personal to you and your circumstance and questions I have heard over and over from the people I know who have lost someone.

If someone struggled here and had a difficult life because of mental illness, criminal activity or abuse, or if they died by suicide, family and friends might worry that their soul will go to Hell or be in limbo. It can be very hard on those left behind if they believe their loved one is still continuing to suffer after their death. We won't really know anything for sure until we ourselves die, but it would be a good thing to do some reading and research on this subject and come up with your own conclusions.

Speaking to the clergy in your place of worship might help too. Don't be afraid to question the things you've been taught. Do those beliefs still work for you, or are they causing you pain? Where did those beliefs come from? How certain are you that they are true? Just because someone is a religious figure doesn't mean everything they say and believe is correct.

Just like with everything else related to grief, these beliefs are very individualized. You have to decide what you want to believe and what will give you comfort. My personal opinion is that I do believe our soul survives death and I do believe there is some sort of afterlife. It gives me comfort and hope that I will be with my daughter again someday. It also makes me feel like maybe she is still around me and honestly, I love that idea!

I also believe we are accountable for the things we say and do while we are alive. I do not believe in eternal punishment like some religions and cultures talk about, but I do think there is some sort of judgement about what kind of person we were during our lifetime.

If you think this idea of a soul is all baloney, and you don't believe God exists, then that's fine, too. There is no right or wrong answer to the question of the soul. You get to decide for yourself and if someone believes something you don't, then that is their decision and what works for them.

In the meantime, your beliefs need to get you through this difficult time. As long as it gives you comfort, then great! It is always a good idea to be open minded though. People believe all kinds of things and some of them are way out there, but that is okay, as long as it doesn't affect you or hurt anyone.

Numerous people I have talked to told me they believed they saw their loved one after they passed either as a flash or a shadow or out of the corner of their eye. They could have seen something outside somewhere or walking down a hallway or at the end of their bed during the night. Other people have said they were getting out of their car and got a glimpse of someone that looked like their loved one and they did a double take. That is their belief, and who are any of us to say it's untrue?

My friend's cousin told me her brother appeared for a few seconds in a crowd she was in for a concert. She had a couple drinks and was unsure at first of what she saw, but said later she knew her brother had been there. Plus she told me, he liked the band she was there to see and it gave her comfort knowing he came along with her, even in spirit.

Some people claim they can smell smoke or cologne or hear different sounds like a bell or music. It's usually something identifiable to the family or friends left behind. This might sound creepy to some people, but for the people who get the sign, it can be a big comfort to them.

One of the coolest messages I have heard about was from a woman I know at our support group whose daughter had died in a car accident. This mother had been having an incredibly difficult time and was driving and crying in her car one evening. This was before smartphones and she had a flip phone with her sitting next to her seat. Texting was pretty new on phones and she hardly ever got messages from anyone anyway.

She had been crying out loud to her daughter and asking her why she had to suffer this pain she was feeling and why hadn't she given her a sign? She yelled at her that maybe she isn't really out there and what does she have to do to hear from her? All of a sudden, her phone beeped the way it used to when you got a text. When she stopped at a stop light she looked down. The phone didn't show a return number. All it said was, "Message Received." It was just the words.

Once she stopped her car, she looked at the phone thinking there might be something wrong with it. The text didn't seem to be coming from anyone. Finally after having her husband look at her phone they decided together that it must be her daughter telling them she was okay. She felt relieved and comforted that night believing that the text was really a sign from her daughter. If that gave this mother comfort, then why not?

Since we don't know for certain what these coincidences mean, it's better not to stand firm or be critical of what others believe. We won't really know for sure until it's our time if in fact our loved ones are trying to reach us by giving us signs along the way. If the death of a loved one is new to you, then there might be unexplained things that happen that can change your mind about life and death. You never know.

EXERCISE:

If we go with the idea that we are able to get signs from our loved ones and they can see and hear us, then this next exercise can be something you do with the intention that your loved one is actually watching.

It has become a popular thing to either let balloons go or buy a flying luminarie to release in memory of your loved one. You can order them easily online and there are eco-friendly options, which is very important. Go to a special place that is meaningful to you and your family – the beach, a mountain, a favorite vacation spot or weekend activity. Just make sure it's a safe place to release it since you will be lighting a candle to get it to rise. Then, write a short note or a letter to your loved one. Tell them whatever you want them to know and attach your thoughts to the balloon. You can do this alone or with family members and friends. It's a meaningful way to acknowledge your love for them and do a small ceremony if you chose. It's nice to do this on your loved one's birthday or the anniversary of their death, but you can also pick any day that works for you. It is beautiful and powerful to watch the balloons rise and finally go out of sight. It becomes like our loved one – out of sight, but not gone.

CHAPTER 7

THE VERBS OF GRIEF

Feel
Accept
Share
Hug

There are many verbs that we can all relate to when it comes to grief. Cry, think, run, sleep, blame, apologize, hope, share, ache, pray, analyze, wish, try, breathe, expect, look, compare, eat, drink, dream, imagine, search, feel, reach, love, kiss, touch, believe. I am sure I missed many words and you can fill in your own. To grieve is also a verb. It is an action word since we are actively coping with the loss of our loved one. It is something in varying degrees that everyone encounters after a death.

The Primary Verb of Grief is Feel

Feeling is an action we all have to take in order to fully experience, process and eventually move beyond our grief. To feel a range of emotions is normal and expected. Whatever feelings you have, allow them to happen. It may seem scary, uncomfortable, and painful, but if you try to deny the act of feeling, somehow the pent up pain will find a way out, or it will get stuck in your body and cause other problems over time.

A friend of mine lost her mother to suicide while she was still in college. She got called into the Dean's office at her school one day and he told her matter-of-factly that her mother had killed herself that morning. Of course my friend was in shock and denial. (As a side note, the way the dean told my friend about her mom was beyond callous and insensitive. It is horrifying that the head of a school would have so little empathy.)

She flew home and her father began telling her the details of the funeral. He also showed her the note her mom had written before she died, but it didn't tell her much about why she had killed herself. The next day my friend listened from the other room as her father told people on the phone about what had happened to her mom. She tried to glean any information she could based on what he was saying, but nothing was discussed with her and her sister directly.

From what she heard, she created her own story about what had happened to her mom and that story became her narrative for the next thirty years. Her family never talked about her mother's death or dealt with the pain they were experiencing after it happened. Over the years, my friend had dropped out of school and kept herself very busy and distracted. It seemed like everyone in the family had moved on from the death, so she tried to also. Thirty years later, when she finally realized there were things in her life where she felt really stuck she began the grieving process. She started off by having a massive panic attack in a grocery store and things went downhill from there for a while. She didn't feel when the loss happened, but that didn't stop the feeling from happening, eventually.

One of the things I have learned from my own experience with grief, and from talking to so many other bereaved people, is that the pain will wait for you if you don't deal with it. It waited for my friend for thirty years! That is why it's so important to actively feel your grief the best you can. There is really no going around it or avoiding it — you simply have to go through it. It's no fun, but it is necessary for your healing and for your future well-being.

The Second Verb of Grief is Accept

To accept is not to agree with the outcome of your loved one's death. It means that you have come to a place where you know there was no other possible outcome and that the reality of it was out of your hands. You have to accept actively. It takes practice, and repetition, like push-ups.

Here are just a few of the things I have learned to accept through this difficult road:

1. Accept that your spouse (or anyone else) is not going to respond like you do to the death of your loved one. It's important to respect how they need to grieve and also give yourself permission to do what you need to do for yourself to get through it. My husband and I grieved completely differently. He went back to work right away and had a long drive to his office. From the minute he got in the car, he would cry all the way to work. Then he would turn it off, work a whole day and cry all the way home. Sometimes he told me he would close his office door to compose himself when he was having an unusually difficult time. But he did the best he could to get through each day.

2. Accept that you are still alive and going to stay that way. I did not have a job when my daughter died. She was my job and when I lost her, I believed I lost my purpose and reason for living. Unfortunately I could not will myself to die either. I did try, but I found out quickly that it doesn't work that way.

3. Accept that you need to take care of yourself. Yoga helped me a lot and I made it my mission to force myself to go every day even if I did nothing else.

4. Accept that every day you are alive is a gift, and you are permitted do something with it, even if it's in service of your grief. A good friend of mine asked me what I was going to do with my time now that I didn't have to take care of my daughter. First I cried, then I told her I had bags of pictures I wanted to go through (that was before the digital age), so she invited me to come over and bring my pictures and we would make a scrapbook. That really became my therapy for the first two years.

I looked at pictures and wrote about my daughter and cried and cried and cried. In the end I had two big scrapbooks full of pictures and memories from her life. The time working on those scrapbooks saved me, and I am indebted to my friend for making the suggestion and letting me go through my grief process. I realized as I made the scrapbooks that I needed to know my daughter's life made a difference and that people would never forget her. That became very important to me and I know when someone loses a child that is what every parent wishes.

You need to decide for yourself what you are drawn to that might get you through the hardest days. Think about what your interests might be. I am sure you will be able to think of something.

5. Accept that you might need help, then accept the help. Let people do things for you! Our friends and

family feel helpless because they can't make us feel better and they would do anything for us if we just asked. Of course, you should ask for things within reason. Most likely they would be relieved and happy to bring a meal, go to the store for you, pick up your child, run an errand with you...the list goes on. I really don't like to ask for help but I learned that sometimes not only is it okay but it was necessary for my survival. In the end I appreciated the help and my friends were relieved they had a job to help me other than watching me cry.

The Third Verb of Grief is Share

An important thing to remember when we talk about sharing is our friends and family cannot read our minds. They don't want to ask us anything about our loss for fear of upsetting us, which is ridiculous since we have our loved ones on our minds night and day, right? In my grandparents age it seemed that when someone died it was out of sight, out of mind. No sharing was happening then. People were not supposed to talk about death or feelings for fear of upsetting the bereaved. But things have changed and my suggestion is to share with your friends and family what you need.

Do you need space? Do you need someone to hug and cry with? Do you want to tell stories about your loved one or look at pictures? Tell them!! And it is okay if you are crying while you are telling them. It is to be expected. They might not be too comfortable when you cry, but if they are good enough friends or family they will let you do what you need to do and still be willing to help.

I needed to tell my friends and family it was okay to talk about their kids in front of us, but I also warned them it might be hard for me. I wanted to still be invited to parties and events that my friends were having but also told them I may not come. I reminded them I still wanted to hear about their kids, even though I knew it would be difficult. When it was too much, I told them. I asked my friends and family not to be freaked out when I cry because I needed to get it out and that helped them accept that it was what I needed to do right now.

I also assured them that I wanted to talk about my daughter. For me it felt very natural and I wanted them to know it was okay to bring up her name. Sharing with them what I needed made it easier on them and on me.

Bonus Verb of Grief: HUG!!!

A hug is something everyone needs even if they are not grieving. Try to engage in the act of hugging every single day. Studies show that hugging someone actually has many health benefits. It can raise oxytocin levels which can help heal feelings of loneliness, isolation and anger. A prolonged hug can lift your serotonin levels which can help your mood. And it also helps boost your immunity, which could be compromised due to the extreme stress you are under because of the loss of your loved one. A hug is a great way to comfort someone who is grieving.

Not everyone likes to be touched, but for most people hugging is an important thing to do. It can help to comfort you while helping your mood and your health.

Hopefully your friends and family are huggy like mine. That always makes it easier. If not, attempt to get them to hug you at least once each time you see each other. When you're comforting a child, hugs are really important for them and for you. Hugging a child can sometimes feel less awkward than hugging another adult, and just like we need hugs in times of need, kids especially need them. It helps make them feel safer and gives them additional comfort during this difficult time for the family.

One More Bonus Verb

I struggled with whether the next verb was more a Noun or a Verb of Grief, but I realized, it is an action word. It is not just a thing, but something we actively do in our grief, and that is: we Dream

Dreaming is something that comes up quite a bit for people after a loss. For some, you could be lucky enough to have happy dreams about your loved one right away. If you remember your dreams, that can be a big blessing. For others, it takes months or even years to remember a dream with their loved one in it.

Some people feel like their loved one was in their dream, but then they can't remember any details when they wake up. Some have stress dreams where the people left behind can't get to their loved one. And still others believe that their loved ones come to them in their dreams as a visitation.

Not everyone agrees with this idea, but I have several friends who have had such vivid dreams, where they felt their loved one was there and believed they got a message from them. In these situations, they couldn't help but feel like they were really with them.

For some people there could be recurring dreams about their loved one, especially if there are unresolved issues around their death. The dreams can be stressful, scary and not welcome at all. And not every dream is giving us a message. Some dreams are just our biggest fears coming out while we sleep.

It can take some time to resolve some of the issues you have surrounding your loved one's death. Your dreams will change as different issues come to light. If you remember your dreams, try to write them down. That way you will be sure to remember and might be able to piece together what you are struggling with. Also, try to be open to the idea of your loved ones coming to you in a dream. It can be very comforting and helpful for your healing.

In the twenty one years since my daughter's death I have had one dream that felt like a visitation. I have dreams about my daughter once in a while, and to be honest, sometimes they are stressful. Other times it feels like she never died and is just with the rest of our family. But these dreams are always fuzzy and don't always make sense. They were never clear and organized like this one dream I had.

This dream happened ten years after my daughter died and it was not like anything else I had experienced before. It was so clear that I remember how my daughter looked and felt. I could feel her weight, since I was holding her and could also feel her body against mine. In the dream she gave me something and I remember how it felt when I took it and the feeling I had when she gave it to me. I woke up feeling emotional and a little out of it, but it was amazing and I was so grateful for the experience.

I have experienced all the verbs listed above at some point during my grief journey, which brings me to another action word that is crucial: Hope. If we don't actively hope, we might never get over our grief. Somehow believing that things will get better is what gets us through the worst of our pain.

I believe we are meant to feel the pain of grief, but then we are meant to love and appreciate our lives even more because of our pain. That is what I actively hope for you.

EXERCISE:

Make a dreamcatcher. The idea of this came from Native American culture and it is a project you can do for just yourself or with the whole family. A dream catcher is a round netted fixture with feathers and beads hanging off of it that can be mounted on a wall, hung in a window or placed above your bed. You can buy these online or at a craft store. Also there are websites where you can get the materials to make them yourself.

The Ojibwa (Chippewa) tribe believe that good and bad dreams flow freely during the night. The dream catcher is there to catch the bad dreams and let the good dreams flow through. It is a lovely idea if you are having trouble sleeping or want to make something meaningful. My wish for you is that your dream catcher keeps all the bad dreams away, and allows the beautiful, peaceful dreams of your loved ones to ease you through your grief.

CHAPTER 8

THE AUXILIARY VERBS OF GRIEF

Would'a
Could'a
Should'a

One of the most advanced concepts in any language is how to conjugate the verbs for actions that did not take place. Something you did not do that you wish you had or something you did that you wish you had not. Some languages don't even contain words for would, should and could, concerning themselves only with discussing things that actually occur, living in the present, only focused on what did or did not happen, not the alternate timelines that might have been.

Sadly, often, there is a strong intersection between the language of Grief and the language of Regret, and in the language of Grief, these auxiliary verbs are almost inescapable.

In the bereavement support group that my husband and I went to after our daughter died, the group talked about the "Would'a, Could'a, Should'as" that every person who has lost a loved one goes over in their minds. It's not a new concept, but it is worth sharing that we've all deliberated all the painful decisions, words and memories with the thought that things could have been different, if only....

For example, "If I would have gone with him in the car, he wouldn't have died," or "If I could have just gotten through to her that drugs are dangerous, she could have made a different choice," or "I should have told him I loved him before he left the house." That one is a big one and something I hear often.

The last conversation you have with your loved one before their death can get stuck in your mind as if it's the only conversation in your relationship that ever mattered. I have heard every variation of this narrative and I know from personal experience these thoughts and words can eat you up inside!

A friend of mine went on vacation several years ago to a popular resort with her husband and three kids. They had been to this location before and were having a wonderful time as usual. Their teenagers decided one night to go out with some other kids they had met so my friend and her husband decided to make that evening a date night for them. They watched the sunset as they walked on the beach and then stopped to have a relaxing dinner.

After dinner, my friend was still feeling like she wanted to do something and convinced her husband to come to the movies with her, even though he felt tired. He really didn't want to and she reminded him he could nap in the movie if he needed to. Plus, she told him convincingly, she really wanted to go, and how often do they get to go out on a date anyway? Her husband reluctantly agreed and they got their tickets and sat down for the movie. Then the unthinkable happened. Halfway through the movie her husband had a massive heart attack and died right there in the theater. In that moment my friend's life and the life of her family was changed forever.

Later, after the shock of what had happened wore off, she began to go over the conversations she and her husband had that evening he died. She wondered why she had pushed him to come with her to the movies even though he had said he was tired and didn't feel like it. What if they had just gone back to their room? Would he have lived? Or maybe he was feeling bad already and he didn't tell her. She told herself she should have sensed something was wrong and taken him to the medical clinic in town. She had grown impatient with him when he was dragging his feet about coming along with her to the movie. Now she felt guilty at the way she had talked to him. Plus, she didn't get the chance to tell him she loved him that night and was grateful for this family trip. She was feeling awful and guilty and confided in me about everything that was swirling around in her head. All these *what ifs* were driving her crazy!

Sometimes, after someone dies, people have unfinished business that never got worked out with their loved one. It could be a conversation that ended badly or an actual event that leaves us feeling unsettled. Whatever it is that's on your mind still needs to be expressed. If you are experiencing that, now is the time to address it.

EXERCISE:

Write a letter to your loved one. There may be any number of things you wish you had said to them, and even though they are not here physically, writing to them can help you unload your feelings and make YOU feel better. You obviously can't send the letter, but if there is something you want to say or ask, write it down. There is something very cathartic and healing about getting your emotions down on paper.

You can write the letter and put it away to look at later or you could hold a ceremony and burn it in a safe place. You could also share it with someone who is close to you and your loved one and maybe discuss the feelings you wrote about with them. Writing your feelings down on paper can release you from some of the burden you are feeling. It won't solve all your problems or take away all the pain, but it is a small step in the right direction.

It is so hard to let go of the control we think we have in our lives. Sometimes the events that lead to the death are due to a horrible accident or an intentional situation. It's difficult to let go of thinking you or someone else caused your loved one to die. If someone did cause the death, it still doesn't help us to change the inevitable outcome. We are just left with the intense feelings of the unfairness of it all. Nothing we said or did or didn't say could have changed the outcome of our loved one's death. Even if we go over every detail of our loved one's death in our minds, with the hope the situation were different, it unfortunately won't change anything. It will drive us crazy though. We have to try to remember as much as we hate what happened, the situation of our loved one's death is really out of our hands.

It's okay and very understandable to want things to be different. That is totally normal and it's something we all grapple with. The night before my daughter went into the hospital for the last time, we had had a really difficult day. She had been really cranky and difficult and I was not happy. She didn't want to eat and didn't want to take a bath, and she wouldn't go to sleep. I had grown impatient with her because I was kind of at my wit's end and I was exhausted! Of course then she went into the hospital the next day and I felt like a horrible mother.

How could I have not known she was sicker than usual? I beat myself up for quite a while thinking I should have known she wasn't feeling well and something was really wrong. She didn't feel well a lot, but why didn't I realize this night was different? Why was I so impatient with her? Why couldn't I have just kept my cool and hugged her all night? After I processed my guilt (and that took a long time), I realized we are all human and we all make mistakes. Also that last night didn't have to be the only part of our relationship that was important.

My daughter and I had amazing days and such great memories. I had to remind myself that our relationship was not based on that last night she was home. I forced myself to not focus on that one evening that was tearing me up inside. It takes a while and it took a while for me, but it is possible to train your mind. Whenever that memory came into my mind I chose instead to remember a funny memory or one that my daughter was happy and laughing.

I have learned over many years to let go and surrender in some instances because it is really all we can do when certain events are happening in our lives. It is a hard thing to face and come to terms with surrendering, but it's necessary eventually for healing.

There are some things that happen that we will never understand and that's okay. We have to somehow let go of the guilt and the feeling of responsibility for our loved one's death. Of course, it's easier said than done. Some circumstances leave us beating ourselves up over our decisions and choices made. It is one of the hardest issues you will deal with as you go through this journey. Talking to a professional or even a friend may help you. It is important to try to talk to someone if these intense feelings continue to swirl around in your mind.

One example of having no control happened to me a few years ago. I was driving in my car and sitting at a red light on a busy street. Coming towards me in the lane going the other way was a truck carrying several of those big dumpsters that people rent when they need to get rid of a lot of trash. The truck passed me and all of a sudden I heard a very loud crash. The ground shook! One of the dumpsters had fallen off the truck about two car lengths behind my car and landed in my lane! Thank goodness no one was waiting behind me but it crossed my mind so clearly in that moment that it was not my time. Had the dumpster fallen one half-second earlier I would have been a pancake. And thank goodness no one else was around to get hurt either. Unbelievable!!

That experience made me see so clearly what being in the right place at the right time means. I literally said a little prayer thanking God it was not my time yet. If you think about the events that led up to that fateful day or night that your loved one died, control is really just an illusion. It's a hard thing to accept and one that may take time to resolve in your mind and in your heart.

In the beginning after a loss it's harder to reconcile why our loved one died. A lot of times, rationally, the circumstances of the death just don't make sense. Some people wrestle with the question of why for the rest of their lives.

But for some of us, it takes going over the circumstances in our heads, talking with a friend or loved one and crying as much as we need to for as long as we need to to get to a more accepting view.

If you believe in God, a higher power or a universal force, letting go of control might be a little bit easier. Some people get a lot of comfort and believe it is God's will or the universe has a plan. But you don't have to believe in God or any big force to realize we don't have a lot of control over anything but how we respond to our situation. It is a tough lesson to learn and accept but one that will bring us more peace.

It's okay and normal to question and not like the outcome. It's okay to be angry and sad and heartbroken, but the hard work for you is that then you need to work on releasing yourself from the blame you feel and the blame you place on others. It takes focus and work on yourself to get to a more accepting place. Accepting doesn't mean you like the outcome or you wanted the outcome. It just means you surrendered to the point that the thoughts and emotions around this are not eating you up inside.

Getting to that point can be done over a lot of time. It also requires talking with friends or family, or you may need to see a professional or a religious leader to help you work through your feelings. Take as much time as you need. This too shall pass.

EXERCISE:

Sit somewhere quietly, preferably alone and think about your loved one. (That won't be hard to do.) What comes up for you? Obviously sadness, but do you feel guilt or anger? Pain? Now where do you feel it in your body? Is it pounding in your head? Or hurting your heart? Do you feel it knotting up in your gut? Try to locate it. Hint: It can settle in more than one place. Once you locate it...

1. Imagine wrapping that ball of feelings up tightly and holding it inside your body.

2. Now imagine your love for your loved one. Let it grow inside your body.

3. Try to visually wrap that ball of feelings with your love and with the love of your loved one. You may cry through this whole process. It is ok to do that.

4. Don't forget to Breathe!!!

5. What happens to the ball of feelings? Does it get bigger? Smaller? Break into pieces? Move?

6. If you're feeling guilty, talk (in your mind or out loud) to that ball of feelings. What would you have done differently if you could do it again? What are you sorry for? What do you want to say?

EXERCISE - Continues

7. If you feel anger, even anger at your loved one; tell them (to yourself or out loud) why you're so angry. What would you have wanted to happen instead? Yell if you need to.

8. When you're done talking to yourself or yelling to your ball of feelings, calm down and take several deep breaths. How do you feel now? Does it feel the same? Has it changed?

9. Now imagine your ball of feelings, still wrapped up, gets surrounded by light.

10. Picture that ball of light and feel it getting lighter in weight.

11. Then imagine it lifting out of you and away from you.

12. Ask your loved one to take it or send it out to somewhere far away.

13. Now sit and breathe.

How do you feel?

CHAPTER 9

THE NEGATIVE FORM

No
Non
Nyet
아니다

When learning any new language, after learning how to say what things are, what they do, and how they work, you quickly learn how to say what they are not, what they don't do, and how they don't work. This is called the Negative Form, or the Negative Structure.

Sadly, the language of Grief has a very specific Negative Form, and that is the negative feelings you might experience when those around you speak or react in a way that does not lessen your pain, or worse, adds to it.

One issue that comes up as we speak about grief is not all of our friends and family want to hear about our loss and be with us in our grieving. They might be supportive in the beginning, but after a while, most people want to move on and pretend like all is like it was.

Over the years I have realized that some people have very limited capacities to cope with difficult situations. It makes them uncomfortable, and even though you are the one dealing with a death, they may avoid you, change the subject when you try to talk about how you're feeling, or maybe criticize you for not moving on with your life. All these reactions have everything to do with their coping skills and not a lot to do with what you actually need from them.

In my own experience, I was surprised how some friends really went out of their way for me when I was just starting out in my grief process. They were supportive and loving and I am so grateful to them for that. I was equally surprised and saddened by a few close friends who could not handle the enormity of my loss.

For example, one person who I am no longer friends with actually said to me, "I don't call you because when I think of calling you, I think of your daughter, and that makes me sad. So I don't call you because I don't want to be sad." I am paraphrasing, but this is what I heard from her. At the time I was incredibly hurt and sad to lose her as a friend, but I didn't have the capacity myself to help her go through MY grief process. I understand now that she just didn't have the coping skills to handle all the pain I was going through.

My life had been shattered into millions of little pieces. Shards were everywhere and I was barely functioning. There was not a whole lot more I could have said to my friend at that time. It may not have been her fault, but the timing was not right to put effort into our friendship from my end. Unfortunately not all relationships survive. It is a sad fact but also, as you are changing because of your loss, your needs and relationships might change as well. Depending on the closeness of the relationship you're struggling with depends on how much time and effort you want to put into keeping it.

Through the years I have learned to be more forgiving of people when I see they cannot handle a difficult situation. But as you navigate this treacherous road, keep your supportive friends close to you and the ones that are not as supportive, realize they are trying the best they can, but they may not be able to give you what you need at this time.

Often negative feelings are brought up by well-intentioned people trying to say things they think will make us feel better while we are grieving. "It's was God's will," or "God doesn't give you more than you can handle," or "You wouldn't want your loved one to suffer anymore, would you?"

In our support group we've heard every variation of this. Another thing my husband and I heard all the time was, "At least you have more children," or "You're lucky you are young and can have more kids."

I have come to realize that people really think they are helping and being supportive with the things they say, even though we know that is not the case. There is not one really good response that I can share with you, but here are a few suggestions on how to respond that I have used in the past:

- "I don't really feel that way right now."

- "Thank you for your opinion, but that is really not helpful for me at this time."

- "I am just trying to take it day by day."

- "Right now, God and I are in an argument. We are trying to work it out"

- "I am grateful for my other kids. But this loss has left a gaping hole."

How careful you need to be about answering depends on how much you care about your relationship with the person you are talking with. If you want to have a discussion, here are other ideas you could say. "I am not sure how I feel about God right now. I am really struggling." Or, "What I really need from you right now is....." It could be support, non-judgment, a hug, or any number of other things.

For a time, when people would say dumb things to me, I would walk away because I felt I might say something I would regret later. Now I can hear these phrases and take a deep breath and send them a prayer that they should not have the pain I do.

It reminds me constantly that people really don't know what grief is like until they have to go through it themselves. It also shows the different emotional capacities of some people to handle the negative things in life.

Grief and Marriage

Grief in general puts a lot of strain on relationships, especially a marriage. If you have lost someone and your spouse has not, it can be a stressful time in your relationship. My friend was taking care of her mom before she died and she told me she just didn't have the energy to deal with her husband when he got home from work at night.

After her mom died she was heartbroken and cried all the time. She just wanted to be left alone. Her husband had become resentful of her time away while she was caring for her mom and now he wasn't sure how to support her in her grief. They ended up going to a marriage counselor who helped them understand each other's points of view. For them, this helped tremendously.

Seeing a professional if your relationship is feeling overly strained may be a good idea. It might help you to understand each other better. You can also talk to a mediator, or your priest or rabbi, if you have a relationship with them and feel like they would be a safe person to open up to. You both have to decide to make your relationship a priority. If you do, then you will get through this. Remember, as much as we love our spouses, we can't read their minds and they can't read ours.

If you decide that seeing a professional is not for you, that's fine, too, but try to keep communication open. If your spouse lost a loved one, you really need to try emotionally to put yourself in your partner's shoes and try to understand their pain. That's a good exercise to understand better where they're coming from and it can help you to find a way to support them.

I am a big fan of making lists. Ask your partner if you are not communicating well to either write down their feelings, if they are not getting their points across, or make a list of what they need from you. That way it will help both of you. If you are the one grieving, then remember that your partner may not know how to support you. You have to tell them what you need from them!

Try to be open as much as you can. That way your partner will not feel shut out and you may get support from them if they know how to help you. And please remember to hug each other for a full minute a day. (Just a hug, folks…) You will be surprised how much a hug can relieve some of the stress you are both feeling and it may make you feel closer to each other as well.

Grief and marriage if you have lost a child

One of the most negative things that can come out of losing a loved one is the stress it puts on marital relations.

When my daughter was born, both my husband's and my focus went to her. Those first few months we went from being in the hospital to coming home to having surgeries and more doctors' appointments than I can count. We were both so exhausted mentally and physically that we really didn't talk about us or anything other than how our daughter was doing and how to make her comfortable. A lot of the time we were in crisis mode, so our relationship was very much on the back burner.

After she died, it was so obvious right away that we were going to grieve very differently. My husband got quiet at home and wanted to watch TV and be left alone. He cried in the car on the way to and from work and cried a little at home, but not much. He couldn't live in grief all the time.

I cried all the time and slept and went to yoga and wanted to talk about my daughter with anyone who would listen. I also looked at pictures of her. My husband couldn't look at them. I didn't feel like doing anything else and I think he avoided me for a while because I was really a wreck. There was nothing either of us could have said to each other to make any difference about how shitty we were both feeling. Neither of us had the strength to hold each other up, which is usually the case when couples lose a child.

I think the reason our marriage survived is not because we are so strong and amazing, but because we gave each other space and permission to each grieve how we needed to.

There was definitely a period of time where we emotionally separated for a while. Because grief takes up so much energy and headspace, it was a choice on our part to figure out how to come back together and it was a gradual thing for both of us. We had to work hard at it by talking to each other, spending time together, being patient with each other's moods, and being really open with how we were feeling. The support group helped a lot, too, by reminding us that all the feelings within our relationship were normal. Looking back, we both agree that we never considered separating or getting divorced at that time. Honestly I don't think we had the energy for that anyway.

We gradually began scheduling some time with family, friends and each other. We began with date nights. We would take walks together and that was a good time to connect and catch up. Eventually we looked at the scrapbooks I had made together and that was one of the first times I remember we really cried together. It was a difficult time for both of us.

Do your best not to make any big decisions about your relationship for the first year after a death. There are so many changes and emotions and even though it feels like things will never be right, things are always changing. It would be good to give yourself and your relationship the time it deserves to try to heal the deep wounds that are caused by grief.

Here are some tips that helped me:

1. Agree to disagree
2. Know that it is normal to have different feelings at different times.
3. Make sure you make time for each other, even though it might feel hard and uncomfortable.
4. Listen without judgement, cry if you need to.
5. Everyone is on their own timeframe, so be patient.
6. Hug each other a lot!
7. Schedule an appointment with a grief counselor if being together is too difficult.

It is so important to remember that we all handle grief, stress and coping differently. This is most probably the hardest thing you will ever have to go through in your relationship and you can't assume or expect your spouse to grieve like you do. The way they grieve might not make any sense to you, but that is really not for you to decide. Remember that! Just like you would want them to respect your grief process, it is important to respect and not judge them as well.

Communication is so important. Loving each other is so important, Patience is so important in this process. Give yourself time. Give your partner time. You may need different amounts of time. Understand and accept that. Time is required to heal yourself as well as your relationship. At this moment, I am sending strength your way. If you don't have enough for yourself, please use mine. You will need it!

Getting through the holidays

Another negative thing that comes up inevitably after someone dies are the never-ending holidays, birthdays and anniversaries that you, your friends and family have no idea how to deal with. We have touched on this a little bit already. The first year is hard because all the events and celebrations will be a first and have this horrible void, but then they come up year after year, whether we like it or not.

Just hearing the words, "Happy Holidays" or the general language around this time about family and being together can cause someone grieving searing pain. And the holidays last for months! Some people decide they will just ignore the holidays all together. Some struggle with going ahead with the holiday while trying to keep their emotions together. Still others try to make a way to honor their loved one. They might have a chair reserved at their table, will light a candle or eat some of their loved one's favorite food.

I have a picture of my daughter in our dining room. I like it there because it makes me feel like she is with us and it is a reminder for everyone who visits too. Many families like mine want to talk about their loved one during the holiday but some make that topic off-limits. This issue is incredibly personal, so each family has to decide for themselves what they are comfortable with. There is no right decision here as long as you actually decide what works for you. Discuss as a family how you will handle the holidays in your loved one's absence, so that no one's feelings are ignored or trampled.

And you may need to make some concessions so everyone feels heard and supported.

It's okay and normal to take a year or two or five off from a holiday that you used to love to celebrate. At some point down the line it would be good to try to find a way to honor your loved one while you also celebrate the way you and the rest of your family want to.

You are not disrespecting your loved one by celebrating. If anything, it can be a time you can honor and remember them and still enjoy yourself and the rest of your family, at least a little. It is also okay to smile and laugh, although I know that is hard in the beginning. This can apply to any holiday or any other day for that matter. Not only is it okay to laugh and smile, it is important. Your loved one will always be in the back of your mind, but you have the right to enjoy yourself as best you can while you are still on this earth.

Some people I know made a new tradition around certain holidays or their loved one's birthday. As I've shared before, on my daughter's birthday, we like to go to the beach. On what would have been my daughter's tenth birthday, our family went to Disneyland. She loved Mickey and Minnie Mouse and she went to Disneyland only once before she died, so for me, it felt like the right thing to do on a milestone birthday.

During that day, my kids talked about their sister and ate her favorite foods. We also went on the rides she would have liked and stood in line to see Mickey and Minnie Mouse. She would have really loved that! Many of the ideas mentioned in this book are suggestions for honoring your loved one. It is a good time to have a family meeting and talk about making new traditions. Not everyone will be on the same page, but getting the conversation started is a first step.

I also know people who decided to stay in bed all day on certain holidays or birthdays. If staying in bed is as much as you can do that day, then that is what you do. If you are in bed year after year, then it is a good idea to talk to a professional or a supportive friend. Try slowly to do something meaningful for yourself and your loved one. That includes getting out of your room and out of your house. None of this is easy, but coming up with new traditions is a stepping-stone to creating a new normal for you and your family.

EXERCISE:

Exercise: One idea to make the holidays more meaningful is to make an ornament or memento as a family to honor your loved one. You could make one together or each person can make their own. The craft stores have all kinds of ideas for this. Adding a picture is nice too, if that feels right for you. If your house doesn't have a tree that gets decorated for the holidays, you can decorate a frame or a votive holder and make sure it is put somewhere during your holidays where everyone can see it.

CHAPTER 10
PAST, PRESENT, FUTURE

ieri, oggi, domani
ayer, hoy, mañana
어제, 오늘, 내일
yesterday, today, tomorrow

In most languages, you first learn how to talk about everything in the present tense. What is happening here and now, what is and is not. This is an apple. That is a book. We go to the store. As you get more conversational, you learn the conjugations and phrasing to discuss the past, and once that is mastered, the future.

The language of Grief reverses these first two. Upon a loss, it feels like all you are speaking is the past — the person you lost, the things you did together, the life they lived. Over time, you become conversational in the present as you learn to live each day without them. Eventually, you are able to begin to contemplate a future that might feel normal for you, even with your loved one absent from it.

Grief: Past Tense

When we lose a loved one, it is nearly impossible to live in the present moment. So much of our thoughts go to how our life was before the loss, and how we are going to live without them in the future. It is painful at first to refer to your loved one in the past tense. That is almost always a painful transition. Being present takes time and a lot of work as it relates to grief. As I mentioned before, it is normal to go over past conversations or the time leading up to your loved one's death.

It will help as you process your loss to allow these thoughts and feelings to come up and eventually it won't be the only thing you think about as you move through your life. This goes back to Chapter Eight where we talked about the "would'a, could'a, should'as." If only things were different!

At first, your memories can be very painful, as you come to realize things won't be the same anymore. But over time, when things are not as hard, your memories will become a source of comfort as you remember the good times you shared with your loved one.

Memories are an important part of grieving. It is one of the most important things we have left of our loved one. It is as important as our pictures, videos and other mementos. It's also what connects us with them once they're gone. What we had with them can never be taken away and all the experiences and memories will always be there, right under the surface or just tucked away. Our loved one will always be a part of us and part of our family.

Making my scrapbooks and writing about my daughter really helped me get through the worst of my pain. I wrote down the difficult memories and also all the good and fun times we had together.

Here are my best five memories of my daughter:

1. She had the best laugh!
2. We used to watch Oprah together and she would clap and yell when the audience did. It was so cute!
3. When we went out, she waved and said hello to everyone.
4. She loved Mickey and Minnie Mouse and I will always be grateful that we got to go to Disneyland before she died.
5. She used to love when we kissed her neck. It put her in a kind of trance. She would close her eyes and put her head up. It was really sweet.

EXERCISE:

Exercise: Right now, stop reading and make a list of
at least three good memories of your loved one. Go
for five if you can...

1. _____

2. _____

3. _____

4. _____

5. _____

It might be hard in the beginning, but you can think of
things one at a time, and having a list close by will help you
accumulate all the good memories that come up for you.
That way you can go back to your list when you're feeling
unusually sad and try to remember the feelings you had
during some of your good memories. In time, you will feel
grateful for all your memories and will be able to see how
your loved one impacted your life and the lives of others
around you.

Grief: Present Tense

As we adjust to this reality, and as we make it through
the initial holidays and birthdays, a new normal is created.

What does that mean? What was considered "normal" has been taken away because our loved one is not with us anymore. What begins to emerge is how we lead our lives without them, living each day as it comes.

You and your family will have to decide what you want to do as it relates to family time, holidays and events moving forward. One thing that was helpful for me was to incorporate a little something of my daughter in everything we did after she died. It made my husband and I feel better to do that. Another friend of mine used to put their father's favorite music on in the background as her family ate. Someone else we know cooked their mom's favorite dish during holidays. It was a subtle and meaningful way to include their dad and mom.

The big accomplishment immediately after a death is to get through each day in present tense. If you have a routine that you want to stick to, that's great. If it feels hard to imagine your days and how you will get through them, then maybe try to break the day into a few parts.

In the morning it might be a good tradition to be outside for a little while. If you normally drink your coffee or tea at the kitchen table or at your desk, bring it with you outside, if the weather permits. During the day, if you need to go to work or if you are at home, set aside five or ten minutes to yourself to either breathe consciously, walk around the block, make a phone call for support, look at pictures if that helps you, or get a hug from a friend. In the evening you can do the same thing or choose something else that makes sense for you. You know your schedule best and what will help you get through the day.

I have known several people who created a ritual of saying good morning to their loved one and talking to them during their day, even though they can't see them. I was surprised by how many people I know who do this. You can talk to your loved one in your mind or out loud, and I truly believe they can hear you. Even if you don't believe that's possible, there's nothing wrong with talking to them. It's a very common practice and it might make you feel a bit better in the moment.

It would be a good use of time in those first few weeks and months to really think about how to stay present. In starting a new normal, I would say just take one step at a time.

Grief: Future Tense

After someone close to you dies, your life goes on whether you like it or not. There are two specific things that come up as a result of this, and your reactions may take you by surprise. The first is becoming the age of your loved one when they died, or surpassing their age. The other is coming up on milestone birthdays or death days.

I have a friend whose dad died when he was fifty. My friend was a teenager at the time and when he turned fifty himself, he got very uneasy and emotional. It took him a little while to figure out why. He had been at a coffee shop one day and was watching a young son and father interact. All of a sudden he began to cry, something he didn't do very often. He began to imagine what his dad might have been like had he lived and was remembering certain good memories they had together. Also, because his father had died at the age of fifty, he never thought he himself would surpass that age.

It had always been a fear of his that he would die at the same age, or before he got to the age his dad did. So he was pretty relieved he had made it to fifty, but he also became fearful that he might drop dead any minute. Luckily for him, he far surpassed the age his dad was and is still alive today.

If you can relate to this fear, you are not alone. It's very common to not be able to see past a certain age if your loved one died then. A counselor might be able to help you with some of the feelings that come up for you. If you are in a support group, it might be helpful to throw out your thoughts to the group and see if anyone has a helpful suggestion. If you decide not to see someone or discuss it, imagine the people in your family and the friends you know who are past the age your loved one was when they died. Do they have a similar lifestyle as you do? Are they active and healthy?

Picture yourself getting to the same age as your loved one. What feelings come up? What fears? Now picture yourself passing their age and hitting certain milestones.

You can even imagine jobs you might have or watching your children grow up or trips you might want to take in the future. You can also imagine growing old. What does that look like for you?

These feelings you have are very real, but they are also just mental blocks. You might need to silently encourage yourself that you are not your loved one. You have your own life with dreams and goals of your own. Decide that you will grow old. It might take away some of the anxiety that comes up for you.

Another Future Tense moment you may experience is when you realize that your loved one has been gone longer than they were alive. My daughter was only two when she died, so it didn't take long. It struck me really hard when we hit the mark past two years and I was aware she had been dead longer than she was alive. It felt strange and very sad for me for quite a while.

Also, when my other children were born, I was conscious when they turned two that I became more fearful of losing them. Once they actually passed age two I had a tinge of sadness that my daughter never got to the age my other kids were becoming. Now they are teenagers, and I never think of this comparison. But I have to admit, when my friends' kids hit certain milestones in their lives — a bat mitzvah, sweet sixteen, graduation from high school and college, I was very aware of the void I felt in missing out on those experiences with my daughter.

It's normal to have these feelings and it is part of the process you might go through in dealing with your loved one's death. As long as you don't feel crippled by your emotions, just acknowledge what comes up and know that this is one of the many things about death that we have to grapple with.

In the future tense of Grief, milestone birthdays and death days come up repeatedly. Just like when we hit a decade or three or five after the loss, it's difficult if our loved one was going to be ten or eighteen or twenty-one or thirty, forty, fifty…you get the picture. Something about hitting the big numbers seems to magnify the feelings around their death. It is a bigger reminder of the passage of time.

The same goes for the amount of time they have been gone. A year without them seems impossible immediately after the loss, and five or ten or twenty years is unimaginable. And yet, it will happen. Those years will be reached. I always say time is really strange. Because in a way it feels like yesterday that our loved one died, and in a way it feels like forever ago…right?

I don't really do anything different on the big milestone birthdays anymore, except the year we went to Disneyland when she would have been ten. When we get to the milestone birthday where my daughter would have been twenty-five, my kids think we should go on a big trip. I guess we'll have to see. All I know is the big milestones emphasize the passing of time and that is hard and sometimes can be very painful for you and the family.

Just like with every other event, try to honor your loved one and do something that is meaningful for you. If you choose not to, that's fine too. One year you might decide it means a lot to acknowledge them, but the next year you could decide you aren't in the mood to put effort or thought into it. That's okay. Sometimes the days leading up to a birthday or death day end up being harder than the actual day. I think it's the anticipation of what that day will feel like that gets us all worked up.

Once the day actually comes, it may not feel as bad as you feared, or it could be just as bad as the days leading up to it. And some years may be harder, too, whether you understand why or not.

I realized after my daughter died that I had to deal with losing her every day, so when her birthday came or a holiday passed, it felt like every other day without her — sucky and sad and sometimes painful. The birthday or the anniversary didn't change anything. It was just another day without her. At least that is how I felt.

Now, this many years later, these events don't feel as emotional or painful to experience. You might feel differently or you may be able to relate perfectly to what I am saying. Either way, be good to yourself and if you feel it will help ease the pain, do something on these big days that will be meaningful and helpful for you. It will get easier over time, too. I promise!

There will come a time when the loss of your loved one won't feel as painful and you'll be able to consider your new life and living it without them. Remember that this is a good thing. Embrace it.

A friend of mine had this happen a few months after her husband died and instead of seeing her progress, she called me at the end of the day crying that she was a horrible person and was already forgetting him. She realized that she had gone out with friends and didn't think about her husband the entire day, not even once. She felt she was betraying him, and her feelings of guilt were tearing her up inside.

This is a very normal fear. The feeling of getting back to your life can seem uncomfortable and scary if you feel like you're forgetting the person you love. But I've been through this, as have so many I have worked with, and I can assure you, it's an up and down thing for a long time. Some days are just more difficult and, for no discernible reason, other days end up being okay and even kind of nice.

I know from my own experience that although there is a fear that you will forget your loved one, especially if you are not thinking about them all the time, once your mind is focused on them again, it will all come right back. They will always be there, in your mind and in your heart.

Remember to be patient with yourself. This is new territory and it is perfectly okay to be able to concentrate on other things besides your loss. I believe our loved ones want us to be happy and make a life for ourselves after they're gone. The fact that you actually might have a whole day where your loved one is not the first thing on your mind means you have begun to successfully create your new normal. Please don't destroy that by making yourself feel guilty. You are slowly moving towards living your life with love and joy, even without your loved one in it every day. Good for you! This is a big step in the right direction!

EXERCISE:

If we look at all our relationships we can see that every person we know can teach us something. It might be something positive, like learning to be honest or compassionate. Or maybe it was something we now know not to do. But this exercise is to write down three things you can see that you learned from your loved one.

Think about your relationship with them. It could be you learned something like patience, empathy, or humor…just to name a few. After my daughter died I thought about this. The main three things she taught me (and there are many more) are love, patience and surrendering. If you decide to, give an example that stands out to you. Whatever the lessons are, it will be good to look at the list and see on paper what role they played in your life.

CHAPTER 11

BECOMING FLUENT IN GRIEF

To become fluent in a new language it takes practice, patience, and a lot of repetition. "The greatest challenge in learning a foreign language is the challenge of memory." That is what one textbook says as it relates to learning a new language. Another aspect is pronunciation. Speaking the language of grief as openly as you can, whenever you get a chance, and finding others who speak that same language, will be a good way to help you process all the emotions you are going through, and thus become *fluent*.

Grief comes from the Latin word *gravis* which means heavy, from which we get gravity. Sorrow is defined as the feeling of deep distress caused by loss, disappointment, or misfortune suffered by oneself or others. As you become fluent in Grief, you will experience this heaviness and distress frequently, often outside of your control, and that is perfectly normal. It is part of your path towards fluency.

Grief can be all encompassing. Some people feel the need to reach out and find a support group to speak about their grief and be able to get their feelings out. Others think the idea of a support group sounds dreadful. It's not easy to walk into a group, but it can be very beneficial if you give it a chance. There is something about the connection of a shared experience and being with others who understand how you feel that can be comforting. It might be easier if you find someone to go with you for support. Either way, it is a big step.

Each group runs a little differently, so if one place doesn't work for you and meet your needs, you might want to try another one to see if it's a better fit. Some groups are very structured and some are much more laid back. It depends on who is running it and who shows up. There are positives and negatives to going to a group.

When my husband and I went to our first Compassionate Friends meeting, I dreaded walking into that room. I had to literally take a deep breath and talk myself into the building. There is nothing fun about walking in for the first time, but the one positive I took out of our first meeting is that I wasn't alone. There was a room full of people who felt the way I did and there was something comforting about seeing that the people who had been grieving longer were actually laughing, talking and smiling. They were not huddled in a corner, sobbing — like I had wanted to do that first meeting. Everyone in that room understood how I was feeling and were supportive and reassuring that all the feelings I was feeling were normal.

The one downside to a group setting is not only do you have to listen to other people's stories, which could be good or bad, sometimes you get a person that likes to go on and on without regard for everyone else and it can be really frustrating. Hopefully you will get something out of everyone's story and also have a facilitator who manages the group and makes sure everyone who wants to share gets a turn.

I know in our support group it was always recommended that we come three separate times because different people show up from one month to the other, and the dynamics of the group change depending on who is there. There could be a topic for the night that the facilitator provides or if someone has an issue that ends up being discussed and people can relate to the topic, that might be the issue of the evening. Some meetings can be very somber and others are lighter, filled with laughter as well as tears. You just won't know until you try it. It could be exactly what you need.

Check online or ask around and see if there might be a group that would be right for you. A lot of churches, synagogues and hospitals also have support groups. You also might want to consider a specialized group for your situation. There are groups for loss by drunk driving, loss in the military, loss by terror, cancer support groups, suicide and murder support groups....anything you can imagine. If there is not a local group you can go to, there might be an online group or a blog that can help you connect with other people who have a similar loss. It really does help to talk to someone who has had a similar experience.

If a support group does not sound good to you and you have no intention of trying one, then there are professionals that you can talk to one-on-one. Or maybe there is a close friend or family member you feel comfortable with and can talk to. Not everyone likes to unload on someone, but I can tell you from experience, you need to find a way to get supported.

There is something about talking things out that can be very cathartic in your grieving process. We talked about that in Chapter Six. One person I know whose father died used to walk every morning with another friend who had also lost her father a few years earlier. They both had very close relationships with them and took turns going over their experiences and feelings almost every day they walked. They cried and tried to process what had happened to each of their dads, and they talked about what effect the loss had on the rest of their family. They also discussed with each other the dynamics within their families and how everyone wanted to deal with the loss differently.

They mourned the fact that things were different now and supported each other in trying to find ways to deal with that. They told me months later that just being able to unload to each other every day and talk about their dads really helped both of them get through the worst of the grief process.

Even those who are not as likely to want to open up need support. Keeping feelings bottled up inside does no good for anyone. If you are a man (or a woman) and you don't feel comfortable crying, take a boxing class and get some of that anger and pain out. Or take up running, weightlifting or swimming. Heavy exercise can sometimes have a similar effect in helping to get the pain out of your body. It's hard to be vulnerable, but try to allow your emotions to come out even as you exercise. I promise it will help you in the long run. These suggestions are just a couple ideas to help you get through your loss and talk about your grief. It is better for your health and well-being to take care of yourself.

If you feel like your loved one's death was somehow your fault, these suggestions above might be hard for you right now. As discussed in Chapter Eight, it will be a process to release yourself from the guilt you might feel. In the meantime, try to be easy on yourself. It will do you no good to continue to beat yourself up again and again. Practice letting it go.

I have created the acronym, WE ARE ONE, as a guide to remind you to take care of yourself. I hope this is beneficial for you. It's a little corny, but bear with me.

W- We are in this together

E- Express yourself – share how you are feeling

A- Appreciate and be grateful

R- Rest – sleep and take care of yourself

E- Exercise

O- Oxygen - remember to breathe

N- Needs - don't forget to ask for what you need: love, touch, care

E- Empathy - let this journey make you more sensitive to others, and treat yourself the way you would treat someone else in your same situation – with patience, love and care

EXERCISE:

Go into a quiet room and close your eyes. Take several deep breaths to relax and imagine you are talking to a close friend who is sitting across from you. Imagine what happened to you instead happened to them. They lost someone and you want to support them. Knowing what you do from your loss, what would you tell your friend? What support would you want to give them? What words of advice would they need? Imagine the conversation between the two of you helps your friend a lot and both of you feel loved and supported. How different are your words of support to your friend from your own self-talk? Do you see more clearly what you might need by doing this exercise? Now, practice speaking to yourself like you would a close friend.

Life After Fluency

It is hard to think of anything positive when it comes to the death of a loved one. For a long time after someone dies it's hard to remember anything but the bad. It's bad our loved one died, it's bad the feelings that we have, maybe it's bad how they died…the list goes on.

But I can tell you, twenty-one years after my daughter's death, her life and death changed me for the better. I am a more compassionate and empathetic person. I am able to be grateful for so much of my life and see things I never saw before. I have a better perspective on life and people, why we are here and what my purpose is in this world. I am forever grateful to my daughter for choosing me as her mom.

She has helped me become the person I was supposed to be and I am still continuing to work on myself. If you can't learn from your pain and loss, then you are missing an important opportunity for growth. I know this now, but it came many years after my loss. Going through the initial pain and the continued pain has taught me so much about myself and how I cope in the world.

Even when I was going through my daughter's life and her death, I kept asking myself what I was supposed to be learning from this experience. Why was my daughter born with an imperfect body? Why did she have to suffer with pain and itching while she was alive? Why did she have to go through surgeries and procedures and be poked and prodded? I had so many questions and I still do!! I didn't understand any of it at the time it happened, and some things we went through I will never understand.

For example, why do people have to experience pain? That one I will never be able to grasp. But now, all these years later I have learned to accept and surrender to the many things I don't understand and can't change. It doesn't mean I like it. It just means I know I have no control over the outcome so I have let go a little.

Through this process, I have learned to be more patient and accepting, open and understanding. In the beginning this is not even a question you can ask yourself. You could be in too much pain, and getting through the day will be the most important thing for a long time. But at some point later in your grief it might be an important question to ask yourself. What have you learned from your loss?

Look at the positive things and the negative ones. How has your loss changed you as a person? Has it changed you for the good? How can you help other people going through loss with what you have learned? Do you relate to people differently? It is a process we need to go through to be able to be reflective.

I believe there is a lesson in everything. Another thing to think about is to imagine if your loved one had never come into your life at all. How would your life have been different? What direction would your life have taken if they were never there to begin with? Thinking about this can also give you a better appreciation for your loved one and the role they played in your life. It might be a another way to learn to be grateful as you move through this journey.

One single person can have such an incredible impact on your life. They can change the direction your own life takes. After my daughter died, our support group talked about what our lives would have been like had we never had our children. Even with the difficulties and the pain everyone agreed that they wouldn't have wanted to give up the time they had with their loved ones. I know for me, even though two years was way too short of a time for her to be on this earth, every moment was precious to me.

I believe some time with a person is far better than no time at all. In my own life I can see that I am a different person now because I knew and loved my daughter. I am a better version of myself and even with all the pain I have endured, I would not want one minute to be taken from me of the time we had together.

Your loved one would want you to continue with your life. What better way than to do something good and meaningful in memory of them? Our friends helped us start a foundation in memory of our daughter right after she died. We used the money we raised in memory of her to do good things for kids in our community.

Some people run a race in memory of their loved one, or give to charity or volunteer. If you are not up to that, release balloons or eat your loved one's favorite food and listen to their favorite music. You should do what means the most to you and your family.

If you are still at a place where you feel like your world has fallen apart and you don't see anything good and positive in your life, then start small. Grief can be a slow process, so listen to yourself and decide if you are ready to do some of the suggestions in this book. And if you're not, put it down and pick it up later. I will still be here when the time is right for you.

EXERCISE:

Get a notebook or a piece of paper and try to write five things you are grateful for every day. If you are at the beginning of your journey and you don't feel grateful for anything, start with the basics. I am grateful for my breath. I am grateful the sun is shining, I am grateful for my dog or cat....that sort of thing. Try to do this every day for thirty days. It's ok to repeat some of the things you are grateful for but try to think of other things, too.

It might take a while and it might not feel like this is a worthwhile exercise, but by stopping to really think about this, it focuses your mind for a short time on something other than grief and it helps you become more aware of your surroundings and the blessings in your life. Keep the book or paper somewhere close to you and you can always add to it during the day if you can't think of five things all at once. And you can write more or fewer than five. That is just a guideline.

At the end of the 30 days go over what you have written. How do you feel? Are you able to feel grateful at all, despite the pain you are going through? If even a tiny bit, you are moving forward, and that is a very, very good thing.

CHAPTER 12
QUOTES & KEY PHRASES

When trying to learn a language as challenging as Grief, it's helpful to have a few key phrases to turn to for comfort and guidance. Here are a few that I find inspiring and may be helpful to you. Pick your favorites and repeat them as often as you need or want until you are fluent in this strange new language. There are so many other inspirational words that have been spoken, so don't stop here. Search and find the ones that work for you and add to this collection.

Sometimes, finding words that inspire and comfort you is just the encouragement needed to continue moving forward and learning to live without your loved one.

Ancient Egyptians believed that upon death they would be asked two questions, and their answers would determine whether they could continue their journey in the afterlife.
The first question was, "Did you bring joy?"
The second was, "Did you find joy?"

- Leo Buscaglia

Seeing death as the end of life is like seeing the horizon as the end of the ocean.

- David Searls

I am ready to meet my Maker. Whether my Maker is prepared for the great ordeal of meeting me is another matter.

- Winston Churchill

Live as if you were to die tomorrow.
Learn as if you were to live forever.

- Mahatma Gandhi

What we have done for ourselves alone dies with us;
what we have done for others and the world remains and is immortal.

- Albert Pike

What you possess in the world will be found at the day of your death to belong to someone else. But what you are will be yours forever.

Henry Van Dyke

To fear death is nothing other than to think oneself wise when one is not. For it is to think one knows what one does not know. No one knows whether death may not even turn out to be the greatest blessings of human beings. And yet people fear it as if they knew for certain it is the greatest evil.

- Socrates

Watching a peaceful death of a human being reminds us of a falling star; One of a million lights in the vast sky that flares up for a brief moment only to disappear into the endless night forever.
- Elizabeth Kubler-Ross

Just because you can't
see it,
touch it,
or feel it,
does not mean it's not there.

- Unknown

Our death is not an end if we can live on in our children and the younger generation. For they are us, our bodies are only wilted leaves on the tree of life.
- Albert Einstein

Death is caused by swallowing small amounts of saliva over a long period of time.
- George Carlin

We understand death for the first time when he puts his hand upon one whom we love.
- Madame de Stael

There is nothing certain in a man's life except this: That he must lose it.
- Aeschylus Agamemnon

The death of someone we know always reminds us that we are still alive, Perhaps for some purpose which we ought to re-examine.

- Mignon McLaughlin

Let life be as beautiful as summer flowers
And death as beautiful as autumn leaves.

- Rabindranath Tagore

Death is for many of us the gate of hell; but we are inside on the way out, not outside on the way in.

- George Bernard Shaw

Death is not poison but merely life's final remedy.

-Terri Guillemets

For what is to die but to stand naked in the wind and to melt into the sun?

- Khalil Gibran

Suicide is man's way of telling God, "You can't fire me - I quit."

- Bill Maher

After all, to the well-organized mind, death is but the next great adventure.

- J.K. Rowling

The goal of all life is death.

- Sigmund Freud

Why fear death; tis just as natural
As a tiny baby's birth,
When it's brought from Heaven's portal
To its new home on the earth.

- Gertrude Buckingham

She died that night. Her last breath took her soul, I saw it in
my dream. I saw her soul leave her body as she exhaled, and
then she had no more needs, no more reason; she was released
from her body, and, being released, she continued her journey
elsewhere.

- Garth Stein

There's nothing that death is e'er able to do
But sever the cord that binds the body to you.

- Gertrude Tooley Buckingham

We must be fulfilled in our own most deeply needed way, then
we can pass gracefully and without regret beyond our life on
this earth.

-Terri Guillemets

For death is no more than a turning of us over from time to
eternity.

- William Penn

Death is just another stage of life, although the one you kind
of hope comes last.

- Robert Brault

Death is your dancing soul returning to the heavens.
                                                    - Terri Guillemets

Now he has departed from this strange world a little ahead of me. That signifies nothing.
For us believing physicists the distinction between past, present, and future is only a stubbornly persistent illusion.
                                                    - Albert Einstein

The really frightening thing about middle age is the knowledge that you'll grow out of it.
                                                    - Doris Day

I intend to live forever. So far, so good.
                                                    - Steven Wright

Anyhow, it's not so bad....I mean, when you're dead, you just have to be yourself.
                                                    -Tim O'Brien

Sometimes you never know the value of a moment until it becomes a memory.
                                                    - Theodor Geisel (Dr. Seuss)

How lucky I am that I have something that makes saying goodbye so hard.
                                                    - Winnie The Pooh

You're going to lose people in life and realize that no matter how much time you spent with them, or how much you appreciate them and told them so, it will never seem like it was enough.

Anonymous

Grief is like the ocean. It comes in waves, ebbing and flowing. Sometimes the water is calm and sometimes it is overwhelming. All we can do is learn to swim.

- Vicki Harrison

I think the hardest part of losing someone isn't having to say goodbye, but rather learning to live without them. Always trying to fill the void, the emptiness that's left inside your heart when they go.

- Unknown

You cannot save people, you can only love them.

- Anonymous

It is amazing that the heart makes no noise when it cracks.

- Bliss

But I think maybe there is validity in accepting that a part of you went with the person who died, and a part of them stayed with you.

- Brittany White

Do I choose to wake up every day and grieve?
No. I wake up every day and know a part of me is missing.

- Renee Scrima

Perhaps they are not stars in the sky, but rather openings where our loved ones shine down and let us know they are happy.

- Eskimo Proverb

If there ever comes a day when we can't be together, keep me in your heart, I'll stay there forever...

- Winnie the Pooh

To die will be an awfully big adventure.

- Peter Pan

It's your road and yours alone. Others may walk it with you but no one can walk it for you.

- Rumi

Feelings are much like waves. We can't stop them from coming, but we can choose which ones to surf.

- Jonatan Mårtensson

It's so much darker when a light goes out than it would have been had it never shone.

- John Steinbeck

Life has to end, love doesn't.

- Mitch Albom

FINAL THOUGHTS

This book is a guidebook on how to navigate through your grief. My intention in writing it was to be as honest as I could and hopefully help as many people as possible along the way. I have talked with hundreds of bereaved people about their feelings after a loved one's death, and in writing this book, tried to capture as many nuances, experiences and details as possible, as it relates to grief. There has to be something I missed, and there are always exceptions to any broad suggestions, but I hope you got something from my expertise and my journey.

This is not a professional counselor's view on how to handle the loss of a loved one. It is my opinion on how to survive a very difficult time, with training from a variety of grief organizations and input from many whose grief journeys I have shared.

You may have agreed with all or most of what I've written, and feel like you can relate to the feelings talked about in this book. Then again, you may not see yourself in these pages at all, and may not feel comfortable talking openly about your pain or acknowledging your feelings.

This book is not going to take away your pain. I wish it could, but unfortunately I am not a magician…or God.

Grief is hard and painful and it is a long road to navigate. My wish for you is that you take one day at a time, take care of yourself, and find a way to honor your loved one while learning to live and thrive without them. Grief can be an incredible teacher if we allow it to be.

Sending you light and love as you continue on this journey….xox

Reference Guide
There is a wide variety of resources if you need support after a loss. Going online is the best way to find what you're looking for, but here are just a few great ones to get you started.

All the best to you as you travel this difficult journey.

www.compasssionatefriends.org - This organization is a support group for the loss of a child, grandchild or sibling. There are chapters all over the world.

www.suicidepreventionlifeline.org - This hotline is available all the time if needed.

www.afsp.org - This national organization provides resources, referrals and support events for families affected by suicide.

www.opentohope.com - This organization is an amazing online resource after a loss. They have a newsletter and videos discussing all aspects of grief and loss.

www.thegrieftoolbox.com - This is an online grief support website. They also have support groups in some areas.

www.healgrief.org - This organization is general grief support and also supports college kids if their parent is diagnosed with an illness or dies while they are away at school. AMF- Actively Moving Forward

www.healgrief.org/actively-moving/forward - The branch of this organization supports college students who are going through a loss. There is online support as well as chapters at 200 of the universities around the country

www.taps.org - This organization gives support to families who are in the military.

If you are in the Los Angeles area:

www.ourhouse-grief.org - This amazing organization has a variety of grief support groups.

www.griefhaven.org - This is also an amazing organization for the loss of a child.

www.hopegroups.org - This organization also has a variety of grief support groups.

www.griefcenterforchildren.org - This organization has support groups for children and teens

ABOUT THE AUTHORS

Stacy Parker is a native Californian, living with her husband and two children in the Los Angeles area. She became a grief expert after the loss of her first daughter, Alyssa, in 1997.

Since her daughter's death, Stacy has been involved with The Compassionate Friends (an organization that supports parents after the loss of a child), which she first joined as a grieving parent, then together with her husband began facilitating their local chapter, and ultimately, they Co-Chaired the 2004 TCF National Conference, taking place in Hollywood, California. In July 2012, she was on the TCF International Conference board that took place in Orange County, California.

Stacy has volunteered as a grief counselor at Our House in Los Angeles, written for the online newsletter, Sharing Wisdom, to help support bereaved families, and together with her husband, been a guest on Open to Hope, an online resource for grief. She was also a parent advocate at Cedar Sinai Medical Center, with the Pediatric Palliative Care Committee and the Comfort Care Committee at UCLA Medical Center, and has devoted her time speaking to the medical community at both Cedars Sinai and UCLA about her experience with her daughter in the hospital.

Stacy attended three IPPC (Initiative for Pediatric Palliative Care) conferences as a parent advocate and spoke to the nurses of ELNEC (End of Life Nursing Education Consortium) to help better improve the environment in hospitals for families that need support.

She is on the board of the Children's Hospice Of America Foundation (CHOAF) that helps raise awareness and funds for Palliative Care and Children's Hospice around the country, and is a parent representative on the hospice and palliative care board of the AAP (American Academy of Pediatrics).

Stacy continues to support families whose child has been diagnosed with a terminal illness or has died.

Grief As a Second Language is her first published book.

Valerie Alexander is a speaker, author, filmmaker, entrepreneur, and the CEO of Goalkeeper, a tech startup building micro-social platforms that make it easier to make the people you love happy.

She is a renowned expert on happiness, author of the Amazon #1 seller, *Happiness as a Second Language*, and a nationally-recognized speaker on the subjects of corporate culture, diversity and inclusion, and happiness in the workplace. She holds an honors certificate in the Science of Happiness from the Greater Good Science Center at U.C. Berkeley, and is the resident "Happiness Guru" for the online talk show, *EVOLVE with John Edward.*

Valerie's books include *Success as a Second Language* and *How Women Can Succeed in the Workplace (Despite Having "Female Brains")*. She is the editor and publisher of *Parenting as a Second Language* and *Creativity as a Second Language,* and owns the Registered U.S. trademark on the phrase, "…as a Second Language" for all books in the self-help, self-esteem, motivation and personal growth categories.

Valerie has delivered keynotes and seminars at a multitude of conferences, law firms, companies and organizations, including the Women's Rights National Historical Park, TEDxPasadena, and she was the 2016 Commencement Speaker at Trinity University.

Valerie's career started as a securities lawyer, investment banker, and Internet executive in the Silicon Valley. She left to care for her mother while she was recovering from a brain tumor (Mom is still alive and well!), then moved to Los Angeles where she enjoyed a successful career as a screenwriter, working with Joel Schumacher, Catherine Zeta Jones, Ice Cube, and others. She has written, produced and directed more than 50 shorts, commercials and PSAs, notably the award-winning, anti-bullying short film, *Ballpark Bullies*, and the groundbreaking commercial, *Say I Do,* in support of marriage equality.

Valerie and her husband, writer-producer Rick Alexander, live in Los Angeles, CA, with their ill-mannered German Shepherd, Vegas.

To receive Valerie's monthly *Speak Happiness* newsletter and two free Happiness workbooks, please visit www.speakhappiness.com/hello.

Other Books in the "...as a Second Language" series

Happiness as a Second Language: A Guidebook for Achieving
Lasting, Permanent Happiness

Success as a Second Language: A Guidebook for Defining and
Achieving Personal Success

Parenting as a Second Language: A Guidebook for Joyfully Navigating the Trials, Triumphs and Tribulations of Parenthoo

Creativity as a Second Language: A Guidebook for Discovering, Nurturing and Unleashing Your True Creative Spirit

Made in the USA
Monee, IL
07 June 2021